D1484195

# Allegiance Under Three Flags
# A Memoir

## Sidney Firth
*Sidney Fersht, Haganah 76490*

Allegiance Under Three Flags
A Memoir

Copyright © 2021 by Sidney Firth

Cover design: Caroline Chen

First and foremost, I am indebted to my lovely spouse, Selma Rittle Firth, whose enthusiasm, attention to detail, patience, and guidance made all the difference in fueling my perseverance to bring this labor of love to fruition. At the age of ninety-one, Selma passed away on August 18 of this year. Words cannot express how deeply I miss her companionship, nor the love and affection which endure undiminished in my heart. Though she is gone, she is not. I speak to her every day.

Gordon Prager, fellow resident of Shannondell at Valley Forge, reached out to us two years ago, shortly after he and his spouse, Jo Ann, joined the community. Being an accomplished author and editor, Gordon offered to lend a hand in shaping the manuscript for publication. Thus began our regular "Sundays with Gordon" workshop sessions, conducted in our living room with fresh biscuits, hot tea, and animated recounting of people, events, and living history.

I am indebted as well to our children and their families for their many fine efforts to help me achieve the ultimate goal of formal publication of *Allegiance Under Three Flags.* In the run-up to my one hundredth birthday on March 24, 2021, that has been on my roster of accomplishments sought within the first century of life.

Great thanks to all.

Sidney Firth
December 10, 2020

*Allegiance Under Three Flags*, a biographical memoir and worldview, comprises three parts:

- **FAMILY, YOUTH, WAR**
- **A NEW ALLEGIANCE**
- **THIRD FLAG**

I dedicate Part One, **FAMILY, YOUTH, WAR**, to my dear maternal and paternal great-grandparents. Beset by pogroms in 19th-century Poland, they possessed the foresight and wisdom to instruct their children: "Leave your home. Leave this country. Find a safe place in the world to raise *your* children." I can only imagine how wrenchingly painful it was for them, as they held their youngsters close in tearful goodbyes, to contemplate the likelihood of never again touching, seeing, or speaking to them for the rest of their lives. Such courage, fortitude, and profound personal sacrifice enabled and inspired successive family generations to stand up to the forces of tyranny and oppression – to oppose and if necessary wage war against them – in the unwavering cause of freedom and democracy.

I dedicate Part Two, **A NEW ALLEGIANCE**, to my *Machalnik* comrades-in-arms in Israel's *War of Independence*.[1] As foreign volunteers to the cause of defending the fledgling State of Israel against the forces of denial and annihilation, we were instrumental in writing a chapter of history that lives to this day, some seventy years later. We of the *Machal*, Jews and Gentiles alike, answered

---

[1] "During this period [May 15, 1948, to July 20, 1949] approximately 3,500 overseas volunteers [other estimates range from 4,500 to 4,800], mostly Jews, but non-Jews as well, were also recruited and integrated into the military network. Most of the volunteers were recently discharged soldiers who had served in the Allied armies during World War II. The name chosen, in the autumn of 1948, to designate this group was *Machal*, an acronym of the Hebrew words *Mitnadvay Chutz La'aretz*, 'Volunteers from Abroad' ... *Machalniks*, as they came to be known." – *Machal: Overseas Volunteers in Israel's War of Independence*, Dr. Yaacov Markovitzky (World Machal, Jerusalem, 2003).

the call and thrust ourselves into harm's way without hesitation or belabored deliberation. Honor and duty impelled our actions in allegiance to principle, justice, and flag. Freely and passionately, we put our lives on the line. And precious lives were lost.

I dedicate Part Three, **THIRD FLAG**, to family and future generations. In hope, there is promise.

## WHY THIS MEMOIR?

Why this memoir? Perspective, principle, and duty. At the age of ninety-eight, though I've unhappily discovered the limitations that failing senses impose on one's mobility and interconnectedness, I maintain both an active mind and a healthy regard for the importance of learning from history, recognizing threats to life and liberty, calling out evil in its many guises, and standing up for human rights.

There was a time when I used to speculate in the rear view mirror of time, both on the personal level and in regard to world events. What if England had not welcomed and made a home for my refugee forebears? What if the British government's Balfour Declaration of 1917, calling for establishment of a Jewish homeland, actually *had* been implemented in the aftermath of World War I? What if Hitler, in the early days of his ascendancy, had not been appeased and emboldened at every turn? What if my own upbringing had been different, and my unrecognized, uncorrected vision problems had not stunted my education and limited my socialization? Would I have gone on, eventually, to become self-reliant, learn new trades, fight for my country through years-long campaigns in Africa and the Far East, and return to a nation grappling with societal, political, and cultural flux, on the brink of losing its empire?

Such musings may well be of academic interest, but they are seldom relevant to the choices one must make when in the thick of it, when thrust to the front lines to deal with the 'facts on the ground' – with the unrelenting urgencies of the here-and-now.


As currently related by the chronicle posted on Israel's *Ministry of Foreign Affairs* website, that country's *War of Independence* was waged from November, 1947, some six months before their declaration of statehood, through July, 1949:

It was the bloodiest of Israel's wars. It cost 6,373

killed in action (from pre-state days until 20 July 1949), almost 1% of the *Yishuv* (the Jewish community) – although that figure includes quite a number of new immigrants and some foreign volunteers.[2]

*Some foreign volunteers.* What an epic understatement. 'Volunteers from Abroad' – *Mitnadvay Chutz La'aretz* ( מתנדבי חוץ לארץ) or *Machalniks*, as we came to be called – numbered approximately 4,500 citizens of fifty-nine countries spanning the globe:

> Machal was established through the organizational efforts of the Haganah and the Zionist movement to meet the urgent need for military manpower and to respond to the demand of newcomers and volunteers who were eager to come to the aid of the *Yishuv* and be part of the effort to create and defend a Jewish state.[3]

One hundred twenty-nine of our cadre made the supreme sacrifice as we struggled, successfully, to defend and preserve the newborn state.[4]

On March 1, 1967, having immigrated with my family to America in May, 1960, I became a citizen of the United States, taking my third oath of allegiance to a country under its storied flag. Here and there throughout the ensuing years, I responded enthusiastically to invitations extended by numerous Jewish organizations and synagogues to address assemblies on the topic of my service in Israel's *War of Independence*. Whether the Union

---

[2] Source: *Israel Ministry of Foreign Affairs* website
<https://mfa.gov.il/mfa/Pages/default.aspx>. Total casualties, including military and civilian wounded, numbered approximately 21,400.

[3] Source: *Machal: Overseas Volunteers in Israel's War of Independence*, Dr. Yaacov Markovitzky (World Machal, Jerusalem, 2003).

[4] Other sources place the number of fallen *Machalniks* higher.

Jack, the Star of David, or the Stars-and-Stripes, the core message was invariant: step up, step forward, and answer the call to defend the banners of freedom.

Sometimes that call is not one publicly issued by a governmental or moral authority. Sometimes it is issued by one's own better self, demanding courage and action.

In January, 2015, I received an e-mail from the *Machal* office in Tel Aviv. Chairman Harold 'Smoky' Simon and Secretary Doreen Bliss had invited me to serve as the keynote speaker for an evening presentation of the documentary-style film *Above and Beyond* at the Katz Branch Jewish Community Center in Cherry Hill, New Jersey. The film, produced by Nancy Spielberg, tells the story of pilots both native and *Machal* who flew missions during the Arab-Israeli War.

After the screening, I delivered my address and then took questions. It became readily apparent that few knew of the *Machal* and the pivotal role played by those who had volunteered to stand with Israel. Subsequently, many in the audience approached me to suggest that I write a book relating my experiences, with special emphasis on the role of the *Machal*.

Fortuitously, the bulk of the narrative and much of the research for my story had been written and accomplished some twenty-five years before, when I'd taken it upon myself to create a record for my fast-growing, extended family. I titled the work *My Life Story* and shared it

exclusively with relatives who span the globe. My hope and expectation was that they might benefit from learning the full extent of my journey and exploits, more about the roots of their own ancestry, and turns of events that all too frequently spelled the difference between freedom and oppression, despair and hope, and life and death.

Today, I relate and build upon that story as both objective chronicle and subjective appraisal, not only for the generations of family who will survive me, but also for a public audience, that they, too, might derive value from a unique perspective on world affairs and thereby come to embrace the imperative to act on principle and answer the inner call of duty.

## PART ONE – FAMILY, YOUTH, WAR
### FAMILY
### YOUTH
### WAR

## PART TWO – A NEW ALLEGIANCE
### AN UNEASY PEACETIME
### ERETZ YISRAEL
### THE LEYTONSTONE TURNING POINT
### SIDNEY FERSHT, *HAGANAH 76940*
### THE HOLY LAND
### PASSAGES

## PART THREE – THIRD FLAG
### ANOTHER COUNTRY
### *MACHAL* REUNION
### WHAT ARE THE ODDS?
### ONE VOTE
### THE DISEASE OF ANTI-SEMITISM
### CALL OF DUTY

# PART ONE
# FAMILY, YOUTH, WAR

# CHAPTER 1
# FAMILY

My father's parents, Caroline and Abraham Fersht, died before I was born. I did, however, know my mother's parents, Anna and Abraham Jacobs, who resided in our home for twelve years.

Suffice it to say that if my grandparents and great-grandparents had been able to envision that one day one of their multi-generational descendants would journey to Palestine to join in defense of the concept and reality of a Jewish homeland, how proud they would have been. How profoundly gratified they would have been to be rewarded in that manner for the many sacrifices they would make in seeking better lives for their once and future progeny.

**The Horse Trader**

Abraham Jacobs was a Polish merchant who traveled from farm to farm trading horses. On one such circuit, at the rural homestead of a couple destined to become two of my eight great-grandparents, their daughter, Anna Apple, caught his eye. With a certain degree of parental encouragement and intercession, an arranged marriage was accomplished.

The farm lay within the province of a town Anna and Abraham called *Plolox* – or something similar. The name stayed with me, as they mentioned it often. (Today, the closest fit I can find to the sound of that name is the medieval city of *Plock*, in the center of the country.)

Anna and Abraham began married life residing and working on the Apple family farm. They were blessed with three children, and life was 'good' by low-threshold standards of relative food and physical security – until the pogroms.

## The End of Benevolence

On March 13, 1881, Russian Emperor Alexander II was assassinated at the Winter Palace in St. Petersburg, ending twenty-six years of relatively benevolent rule that had included reform and relaxation of laws and strictures placed upon the country's considerable Jewish population. In the aftermath of his slaying, a resurgence of anti-Semitism shattered hopes and lives as riots and bloody pogroms erupted in many parts of the nation.

The disorders spread to Poland, and before the year was over, Jewish communities and enclaves had been subjected to arson, pillage, rape, and murder.  Some of the outbreaks were checked by the Russian authorities, some disregarded. In others, local troops and police joined in the attacks.   Provincial commissions investigating the root causes ascribed them to "Jewish exploitations." In May, 1882, the government promulgated a series of laws which expelled Jews from many villages and towns.  They were tarred as scapegoats, blamed for the region's unrest, and forced to migrate in order to survive.

Discrimination through anti-Semitism had never ceased to plague and impose hardships on Jewish communities throughout Europe for centuries, but pogroms unchecked by the Polish state during the late 1800s made living conditions there intolerable.

## Flight

For the Fersht and Apple families, there was no choice other than to flee, and hence it was that they, amongst tens of thousands of similarly threatened people of the faith, made their way as refugees to England. In 1887, Anna and Abraham packed their few belongings, leaving behind their three children – Labish, Isaac, and Rivka (my mother, the youngest at age nine) – until they could establish a new life in some foreign country. They traveled in steerage, in the belly of a ship bound for England, where they disembarked in the shadow of the Tower of London.

The Lord Mayor of London, along with the *Jewish Board of Guardians*,[5] formed a committee to raise funds and provide relief for them in the form of housing, food security, and employment opportunities, but the incoming tide quickly overwhelmed the organization. Jewish immigrants were predominantly poorly educated and Yiddish-speaking, further exacerbating the challenge of cultural assimilation and societal inclusion.

Amidst outcries to stem or halt the immigration, Britain turned to America for assistance in the form of accommodating a portion of the influx. The United States, however, having already opened its borders to waves of Eastern European refugees who numbered in the millions upon millions, was unable and unwilling to do so. As a consequence, the flow of huddled masses to the United Kingdom increased, which further taxed the physical and financial resources.

## The Miracle of 21st-Century Genealogical Research

I knew little about my paternal grandparents, Abraham and Caroline Fersht, other than that they were from Klodawa, Poland. My father seldom if ever spoke about them.

In the 1990s, when I was deeply into genealogy, I would check local phone books for the name *Fersht* whenever and wherever my travels took me. In 1993, on a trip to southern California, I looked up and telephoned the home of Ilan and Melissa Fersht. I introduced myself, explaining that my surname *Firth* was an Anglicized version of theirs – and that a family connection was entirely possible.

The ensuring conversation, though relatively brief, was a

---

[5] A charity founded by members of London's East End community in 1859 for 'relief of the Jewish poor.' <u>Source</u>: Magnus, Laurie, *The Jewish Board of Guardians and the Men Who Made It, 1859-1909: An Illustrated Record* (London, 1909).

revelation. Ilan related the story of how his paternal grandfather and the child who would become his father left Poland for Palestine in the early 1930s. I asked if there were any of his Fersht kinfolk remaining in the old country. "No," came the solemn reply. They had all perished at the hands of the Nazis.

In August of this year, during the course of preparing *Allegiance* for publication, I reached out to Ilan Fersht for the second time, again by phone. He was nothing short of amazed to learn that not only was I continuing my pursuit of accounting for the fates of Fersht family members, but also I was well into the process of preparing this deeply personal autobiographical essay. Most pleasantly surprising to him, however, was the very fact that I was *extant* – a living, lucid, driven soul at the tender age of three shy of one hundred!

When I first spoke with Ilan, he was a young man of thirty-six, enjoying a career in the financial services sector. Today, he continues to reside in the same community, practicing the same profession. Yet, somehow, in the blink of any eye, he's become a sixty-one-year-old – and a doting grandfather who has himself spent considerable time building a vast genealogical database and tree.[6]

What is there about one's family heritage that can inspire a person to become part detective, part archaeologist, and one hundred percent devoted to connecting the dots of relatives past and present, far and near? The question readily answers itself: *family*. Blood ties. The awesome chemistry of nature, nurture, and

---

[6] Recently a family member informed me he had researched our Fersht family. He determined that the several hundred who had remained in Poland during the late 19th and early 20th centuries had all become victims of the Holocaust. Remarkably, Ilan Fersht, during the course of our conversation this year, related a virtually identical finding on the part of his brother, who had participated in the annual *International March of the Living* from Auschwitz to Birkenau four years ago on Holocaust Remembrance Day. 'Hello from Auschwitz,' came the simple, chilling text message to Ilan from his brother – followed by photographic copies of four pages of Fersht family names recorded in the Nazi's meticulously maintained journals of the exterminated.

the course of events that makes us who we are, influences how we think and behave, and stokes our ambitions.

## The Farmer's Daughter

Zayda and Bubby, as my maternal grandparents Anna and Abraham were known to us, sailed to England and disembarked in the London East-End knowing there was a large Jewish population already living there. As Yiddish was the predominant language in the community, it made it easier for Jews to make a new life for their families. Zayda had to work two or three jobs as a presser in a clothing factory to make a living.

Eventually, when they had saved enough money, arrangements were made to spirit their children out of Poland. There was no legal way to accomplish this. It took courage, cunning, and a great deal of bribery and good fortune to be successful. The escape was made possible by an uncle who had paid and trusted a farmer to get them out of Poland in a horse-drawn cart. Rivka (Rebecca), my mother-to-be, sat up front with the driver while her brothers Isaac and Labish (Louis) hid under layers of wheaten straw in the rear of the buckboard. At the border, sentries asked the farmer to state his business. He claimed to be transporting feed to a nearby village and introduced Rivka as his daughter. The guards then poked through the straw with their bayonets, narrowly missing the boys. Once across the border, the children were met by the facilitating uncle. How he and the three youngsters managed to cross through Germany and France without papers or passports, I will never know.

## Deprived of an Elementary School Education

When the three children finally arrived in London, the boys were registered for school immediately. But not Rivka. Being a 'remain' – an archaic term for a "leave-behind" – the peasant mentality dictated that she stay at home. Females were considered unworthy of receiving a formal education. The woman's role in life was to marry, bear children, cook, clean, and be there for the

5

husband as a dutiful wife. A male, on the other hand, had to be educated, had to learn a trade, so that he could become a dependable family provider.[7]

Sadly, there are operative vestiges of such cultural and institutional bias to be found yet today throughout the world's mature, industrialized, free-world countries. What saddens me more is that my mother could have made an even greater impact, could have contributed even further to the welfare of family, community, and country, had she been afforded a proper education.

Nevertheless, as she came into her own in young adulthood, Rivka *was* able to rise above her stipulated station in life. She grew to become respected, loved, and admired not only by her husband and children, but also by all those who came to appreciate her strength, character, and wisdom. Quiet-spoken, confident, and remarkably fluent in her second language, English, she was an inspiration to us all.

She and my father, Davis Herschel Fersht, were blessed with nine children. Celia, the eldest, was twenty-one years my senior. Next in order came Freda, Hettie, Alfred, Joseph, Susie (Sue), Judah, and Kitty, who was two years my senior. Today, I am the sole surviving sibling. May they all rest in peace.

## The Family Name

Both Rebecca and Davis had been deprived of an elementary school education in the U.K. For father, reading, spelling, and transcribing the spoken word into the written were lifelong challenges. Ergo, in reporting the birth of each of the nine Firth siblings to the *Register of Births and Deaths*, he typically accepted the clerk's interpretation of the sound of the family surname. "Is that spelled F-I-R-S-H-T?" he'd be asked. *Yes.* "F-A-S-H-T?" *Yes.*

---

[7] Rivka was eventually dispatched to a factory, learning to make buttonholes by hand to help support the family.

And so forth. My birth certificate reads *Firsht*. Their tombstones read *Fasht*.

In case those conditions hadn't produced more than enough confusion for me regarding the family surname, when World War II was declared in the U.K. after Germany's invasion of Poland, the food and consumer goods rationing program bureaucrats entered the name Sidney *Fersht – F-E-R-S-H-T –* in the program rolls. From that point forward, if I wished to be recognized as a legal entity by Her Majesty's Government, I was obligated to be that person. Fine by me.

# CHAPTER 2
# YOUTH

As a toddler, I had what is commonly referred to as a sheltered existence. My father had learned shoemaking, progressively acquiring the skills to one day establish his own business fashioning bespoke ladies' footwear using the tried-and-true tools of the trade. He became a master craftsman, working long days away from home, consumed in the art of turning leather into durable footwear.

My mother was the homemaker, equally if not more masterful in her craft. She insisted that I stay put, playing alone in our backyard rather than being exposed to the corruptive influences of the neighborhood. She objected strongly to the unsavory behavior of other families' children, who were deemed to be running wild as they cavorted in filth, gambled, cursed, and committed various other misdemeanor sins of youthful exuberance. Nor, given the tacit evidence of their parents' permissiveness, was I permitted to play with them in their homes.

I remember a remark Mum made when I was older: "We may be forced by circumstances to live in this kind of environment, but once we close our front door, we choose to live by higher standards." Such determination and discipline spoke volumes for the principled lady my siblings and I proudly knew as our mother. And yet, her good intentions had unfortunate consequences, since shielding me served also to isolate me from the outside world. I became withdrawn, a loner and, in effect, a recluse.

I recall as if on videotape the day my sister Kitty, two years my senior, holding me tightly by the hand, led me to the Christian Street elementary school in Whitechapel for my first day as a first-grader. We entered through the playground area, swarming with hundreds of untethered kids running freely, enjoying themselves boisterously. I was petrified.

In due course, thankfully, I made my way to my assigned classroom. Holding at least forty children and structured in stepped rows like an amphitheater, it struck me as cavernous. I retreated up, up, up to the remote security of the back row. From that vantage point, I could take it all in: the rowdiness, the mirth, the sense of belonging held by all but me. I peered toward the front as the teacher introduced herself and called for order. I could hear her distinctly, but could not make out her face or the contours of her form for the life of me. Her gestures blurred into a foggy haze. The shock of that realization hit me squarely in the gut: I could not see!

What was I to do? *Wait. Maybe it will clear up*. I clung to that hope, but it was not to be. So I tried to cope and compensate. As the teacher chalked words and numbers on the blackboard whilst teaching a lesson, I would scurry down the steps to try to make them out. You would have thought she'd discern that as a clear signal of the difficulty I was having, but no. At length, frustrated and forlorn, I stopped checking the blackboard.

Exams were my nightmare. Knowing in advance that I would fail miserably, I swallowed the pain and lived with the shame. Never once did any of my teachers, cognizant of my failing marks, question my need for help. To them, I was an outlier. A slacker. A hopeless case.

I waited to see – no pun intended – whether something might happen, some miracle of chance or circumstance, to make things better. Two years passed. It wasn't until third grade that my sister Sue, helping mother in the kitchen, asked me to get her handbag as she pointed to the corner of the room. As I searched awkwardly with my hands, a moment of epiphany came for her and – at long last – for me. "Oh, my dear goodness, Sidney, you can't see a blessed thing, can you?"

With all dispatch, Sue arranged an appointment for me with Hors Opticians, serving the London School District. The optometrist performed the standard array of eye chart and optical device enhancement tests. "It is better like this or – like this? Like this—or like this." On and on until, having completed her examination, she exclaimed, "When was this child's eyesight last checked? He's virtually blind." Shaking her head in astonishment and pity, she wrote out a prescription for me to be outfitted with eyeglasses.

Whether or not Hors Opticians sent an official record of that examination to my home or to the school headmaster, Mr. Solomons, I cannot say. But one would have thought that any reasonably perceptive individual, especially teachers charged with the educational nourishment and the *in loco parentis* responsibilities attendant to the profession, would have deduced immediately from the bespectacled boy in front of them that vision problems had been at the root of his struggles and failures in the classroom. Again, sadly, it was not to be.

It wasn't until ninth grade that I mustered the gumption to call my condition to the attention of school staff, and by then, at age fourteen, events were about to overtake my school life and force me to abandon formal secondary education. Thereafter, through dint of spirit and grit of determination, I became an autodidact: a self-taught journeyman, apprentice, and master of diverse trades that would sustain and reward me throughout the unchartered territories and remarkably diverse journeys that followed.

## My Hebrew Education at Age 7

Rabbi Izenberg gave Hebrew lessons in one of the front rooms of his quaintly Old World European home, across the road from our place on Grove Street. On entering, one encountered the sensation of having been transported to the past, to a humble 17th-century abode in rural Poland, the country from which the orthodox rabbi had immigrated. A crudely fashioned worktable occupied the center of the room. Its well-worn surface and attached bench seating consisted of simple planks cobbled together. Candlesticks adorned either end, providing meager lighting for the long, cold winter nights ahead. That was it: Spartan, utilitarian, and all that one needed to serve the purposes of instructor and pupil.

There were to be no lessons in Jewish history. How could there be? Rabbi Izenberg did not speak English. The teaching consisted exclusively in learning the Hebrew alphabet and phonetic pronunciations of words, phrases, and sentences drawn from prayer books written in the mother tongue, without parallel text in English.

It was obvious to me, as it should have been to anyone, that my Hebrew teacher's prime and only objective was to coach his students for a performance, to enable them to *act* as if they understood the meaning, the import, the gravity of words spoken from Old Testament. Being called to the *bema*, to the synagogue's altar podium, for bar mitzvah readings from the Torah was a high honor in a rite of passage steeped in tradition through millennia. Even as a child stymied by poor eyesight and feelings of isolation, I could appreciate the fundamental value and importance of knowing the *meaning* of my scriptural testimony before the congregation. Instead, I was taught to parrot the sounds of the Hebrew text, to assume the role of a learnèd youth applying for manhood. Is it disrespectful to say that I felt like a trained animal in a circus act? I don't think so.

I do remember attempting to discuss with my Dad the fact that the Rabbi was teaching Hebrew without translation. Father must have considered it acceptable nonetheless, seeing as how his other three sons had had the same teacher and gone on to accomplish the mission of bar mitzvah.

If anything, that experience served to stoke my hunger for deeper learning, for acquiring the tools and knowledge with which to become more self-reliant within a society where distinctions of class, worship, ethnicity, and education mattered greatly.

## Sister Celia's Wedding

At around the same age, I was volunteered by my parents to participate as a pageboy of sorts in sister Celia's wedding. The event holds a special place in my heart. Quite possibly the occasion burns most brightly in my memory and in my heart because it was the one and only time that I got to experience seeing my parents mixing happily with a host of family and friends.

Guests were treated to a lavish array of delectable foods. A lively band filled the hall with the joyous strains of Eastern European Ashkenazi Klezmer instrumentals, and, when the time came, partygoers danced the Hora to the celebratory song *Hava Nagila*. The revelry roared on until midnight, at which time the happily weary and pleasantly intoxicated guests made their way to limousines lined up outside the hotel, waiting to take them home.

Helping to gather whatever uneaten treats remained, I made my way to horse and cart, piled in, and nodded off to the undulating motion and the clopping of hooves on cobblestone as the wagon made its way slowly back home to 28 Grove Street. I felt a hand on my shoulder. "Little man, you've had a busy day."

## The Hazelnuts Casino

There's a saying that goes, "Necessity is the Mother of Invention," an adage that goes all the way back to Plato. Growing up, we knew little or nothing of Greek philosophers, but we were all too familiar with learning to make the most of what we had.

Mum would give Kitty and me handfuls of nuts every day. Employing a shoebox, we would make up a simple game to be played outside with a few of the other kids in the neighborhood. We'd cut a series of holes in the lid of the shoebox, small to large, assigning numerical values to each. The larger the hole, the smaller the number.

From a distance, players would take turns pitching hazelnuts, winning the number of nuts designated if their pitch managed to find its way through a given hole and into the box. The most important part of the enterprise was to find the optimal location. We set our pitch near the streetcorner for high visibility, placing the box near, but not adjacent to, the base of a building wall in such a way that missed attempts would be easy to collect.

Those who came to play brought their own supply of hazelnuts, and as soon as we'd assembled a quorum, the casino was open for play. On a good day, we'd come home with more than we'd started with, but win or lose, all enjoyed hours of excitement and fun.

### Delivering Passover Orders

Dad's brother Morris was a grocer whose home-*cum*-store was located nearby on Cable Street. As a relatively 'mature' nine-year-old, I was asked to help Uncle Morris by making pushcart deliveries to area customers. Compensation came in the form of tips – one pence here, tuppence there. In the old style coinage, twelve pence equaled a shilling, and with ten shillings – representing the sweat equity of about one hundred roundtrips bearing cargo hither and yon – I was able to purchase my very own conveyance: a used bicycle.

As the son of a dexterous master craftsman, I was able to grasp firsthand the creative power and worth that simple tools imparted to those who knew how to use them. Being precociously mechanically minded and a tinkerer as well, I disassembled the bike in its entirety and rebuilt it painstakingly piece by piece, cleaning and painting the frame, lubricating bearings and sprockets, tightening and testing until I was satisfied. I mounted it as one might an unbroken horse, carefully, with respect for its nature and purpose. Starting in the backyard, bracing one hand against the exterior wall of the house to maintain stability, I applied force through my legs and feet, feeding energy into the pedals, round and round, gaining speed in forward motion. In short order, I was able to abandon the psychological security of the back wall and achieve balance all on my own. It was exhilarating. I had wheels. I was one with the bike. With the wind in my face, I tasted a gloriously unparalleled freedom of movement and sense of independence. The entire undertaking served as a confidence-booster and an early indication of the self-taught man to be.

## Difficult Times

Even as I entered grade school, my parents were exhibiting signs of fatigue. Repeatedly, my elder siblings would suggest that Mum see a doctor. Stoically, she'd reply, "Not to worry. I'll take a rest and be just fine tomorrow."

During the 1990s, I periodically visited family and friends in the U.K. On one such occasion, I quizzed Celia about those terribly difficult times, when our parents' health had begun to slide downhill and my as-yet undiagnosed myopia had impeded my social development. How was it possible, I asked, that it took three years to discover I couldn't see? Why, when at last I'd been diagnosed with severe myopia, had the optometrist's finding not been reported to the school? How could parents and teachers not have connected the dots of my inability to focus and lack of depth perception with my predictably failing grades?

Celia reminded me of the adversities our family had suffered at that time. Dad had been betrayed by a brother-in-law, Isaac, whom he'd taken into the family business. Isaac's embezzlement was revealed at first by Celia herself when she spotted anomalies in the keeping of the books. At first, Dad refused to believe Isaac would do such a thing, breaking a commandment made more sacred by the bonds of kinship. At the end of the month in which Celia's discovery was made, however, proof came in the form of a demand by a supplier to be paid for goods already shown as cleared in the accounts. The extent of the crime, which had been ongoing for some time, was substantial – to the threshold of bankruptcy. It broke Dad's heart, and Mum's as well.

Shortly thereafter, Dad had had a serious accident falling off a moving trolley car, shattering his shoulder blade. We had visited him in London Hospital. He was fairly immobilized, with the affected limb propped to shoulder height via a metal harness whose support rod extended from the elbow joint to an anchor at the waist. Our father, Celia further reminded me, had been the family's principal, self-employed breadwinner. With him out of commission, the burden of financial support for our extended family fell squarely on all of the older siblings.

Mother's health continued to deteriorate. Nevertheless, she soldiered on, stalwart and uncomplaining as ever, doing her best to keep house while also tending to her parents, who by this time had become bedridden. As always, she resisted suggestions that she seek medical advice. "A bit of rest is all I need."

Sue, sixth-born of the nine Fersht siblings, stepped up to help ease the burden. Even though relieved of the daily chores, however, Mum's fatigue did not abate. Her weariness progressed to the point where, with her reservoir of stamina virtually depleted, she finally relented and agreed to see a doctor. He had her hospitalized immediately. Breast cancer. It had spread to all parts of her body. Inoperable. We were devastated.

Now Sue was expected to keep house all on her own, taking Mother's place. Even though by then six of our older siblings had married and left the nest, there were our bedridden grandparents to care for, parents who were in and out of hospital, and school age children Kitty and Sidney to shepherd. At the outset, Sue was quite unhappy with her *de facto* role – but she proved equal to the task before her.

## Death Strikes 28 Grove Street

With Old World Eastern European state recordkeeping being relatively lax, especially regarding oppressed minorities forced to emigrate or flee for their lives, it was no wonder we did not know the exact birthdates of grandparents Zayda and Bubby. All we knew when they passed away in 1933 was that they were "very old."

The ritual of mourning for those of the Orthodox Jewish faith entailed having the undertaker – the *Chevra Kadisha* in Yiddish – come to the home of the deceased and enlist members of the family to assist as a blessing – or *mitzvah*. I can see it now, as they covered the remains in a shroud and placed the body in a plain wooden box constructed of unstained pine planking nailed together crudely. The overall impression was that of a humble peasant

15

farmer's crate designed to carry produce to market. Atop the makeshift casket they laid a broad white sheet and placed a single candlestick, lit and flickering in the artificial twilight of the room. Those sitting *shiva* included an elderly man or woman, depending on the sex of the departed, who served as a *Wächter* (in English, a *watcher* or *overseer*), one who prays for the soul of the loved one straight through until the moment of interment.

I was all of twelve, less than one year from being called to the *bema*, and already exhibiting signs of cynicism and rebellion. The ceremonies surrounding death impressed me as being devoid of genuine respect for the deceased. The trappings of ceremony were invariant from one lost loved one to the next. The prayers were formulaic. Where was the recognition and celebration of the individual, of his or her unique anthology of deeds? Our family's bereavement was not eased. Rather, it was, in my eyes, exacerbated.

## The Bar Mitzvah Boy – March 1934

Eighty-five years ago, in March, 1934 – the year that Adolf Hitler arrogated unto himself the reins of power as the German state's *Führer* – I prepared to become confirmed to manhood within Judaism through the rite of *bar mitzvah*. Six years later, with the nation's fate hanging in the balance, I would enlist in the Royal Air Force and take up arms against the forces of fascism and the Nazi peril.

Who could have imagined such maturation and transformation, from preteen child of immigrant parents to uniformed soldier in service to his nation, all in a few short, tumultuous years? Certainly not I, as I dressed that sabbath Saturday morning for the call to the *bema*. Services were to be held at the *Fieldgate Street Great Synagogue* in the East End. Originally going by the Hebrew name *Sha'ar Ya'akov* – the *Gate of Jacob* – the temple was distinguished from other smaller ones on the street through its aptly 'christened' English title incorporating the superlative adjective *great*.[8]

Mighty as it was in that respect, however, the house of worship was not invincible. Founded and constructed between 1887 and 1889, the structure would be bombed and heavily damaged by the *Luftwaffe* during the *Blitz*. In the years following V-E Day, as Londoners rebuilt their lives and institutions, so, too, did the congregation of *Sha'ar Ya'akov* repair and rejuvenate their temple.

The *Fieldgate Street* congregation, including and especially the rabbinical staff, were all strangers to me. Though our family had been longstanding members of *Grove Street Synagogue*, Father and I had for some time been the only ones attending their services, what with Mum sick in bed and the rest of the clan working.

The ceremony proceeded as planned, with me, a puppet on strings, mouthing the words and performing my role. Dad seemed pleased. Another son becoming a *bar mitzvah*. Another tick in the box.

When the service and ensuing processional had ended, I rushed home as soon as I could to my Mum's bedside to try and comfort her and to report how dutifully and well I'd conducted myself. Her adoring smile was reward beyond measure. I stayed and read to her, as I usually did every day after school. I can see it now.

## The First Grandchild

My sister Freda and her husband Morrie had just given birth to our parents' first grandchild, a darling girl named Daphne-Ann. I was in their bedroom when Freda, bearing the swaddled infant, entered and began to attempt to hand the bundle over to Mum to hold. Alas, however, mother was just then emerging from a heavy dose of morphine and was unable to accept the precious gift. The

---

[8] 'Former Fieldgate Street Great Synagogue' – posted online by *Survey of London* (July 2, 2018): https://surveyoflondon.org/map/feature/837/detail/.

scene was a tearfully sad one for all in attendance.

**A Nocturnal Premonition**

By June of that year, everyone knew that Dad was faring poorly. His recuperation from the trolley accident had been progressing slowly, and sometimes in the wrong direction. With Mum fighting a losing battle against her cancer, she and Dad slept in separate beds.

One morning, in the wee hours, Mum awoke, disturbed by an insistent premonition that something had gone terribly wrong. With great effort, she crawled out from under the covers and listened in vain for sounds of breathing or the slightest sign of movement from the inert figure in the adjacent bed. Sensing the worst, she tried valiantly nonetheless to awaken Father, to will the spark of life back into him, but he had indeed – mercifully and peacefully – passed in his sleep. Dead at the age of fifty-six.

Ever the matriarch, and summoning the residue of her physical strength and mental fortitude, she called out to us, instructing Kitty and me to get dressed and notify the family, who lived within a one mile radius of our Grove Street home. Father, we learned later, had suffered a massive coronary infarction.

Five months later, on a typically raw and rainy, steel grey November day in London, Mum succumbed to her illness and joined Dad in heaven. May they rest in peace.

**Orphaned at Age Thirteen**

With our parents and maternal grandparents gone to their eternal rest, I felt incredibly lonely and confused. Even given the heartfelt, eagerly extended supportive bonds of family, including siblings, some of whom were old enough to be regarded as parental by a thirteen-year-old, I felt every bit the orphan. The mainstays of my youth had been cut loose, and I was adrift. The once vibrant residence at 28 Grove Street became a house of somber reflection and unutterable gloom. For months on end, I was required to intone the Kaddish, twice daily. If rote repetition had any salutary effect on my melancholy, it was that of numbness.

During the weeks and months that followed, daily routines of home life and schoolboy obligations carried me forward through the haze. Then, at age fourteen, with my elementary school education having concluded, I was deemed ready to enter the society of the working class. My sister Sue, who had managed the Fersht household from the onset of Mum's illness, was now by custom released from that duty and free to consider marriage.

Sister Celia, twenty-one years my senior, had not been blessed with children. She and her husband, true guardian angels, volunteered to take sister Kitty and me under wing and give up their apartment for a larger one. To call their act of kindness a mere *mitzvah* would be a vast understatement. It was a blessing.

## The World of Hard Knocks

Upon leaving school, I was advised to further my education through evening classes and to report to a Jewish agency where a counselor would situate me in a trade. Whether small workshop or large industrial enterprise, factory life in England during the Great Depression was arduous, frequently dangerous, and reliably bleak.

Nominally a man at thirteen, I was about to enter the world of hard knocks. With prospective employers having the upper hand, my first placement was as an entry-level apprentice to M.P. Davis Furniture Manufacturers. The enterprise was located two miles northwest, at 17 Kingsland Road. A small clutch of journeymen crafted tables, bedroom suites, sideboards, cocktail bars, and other specialty pieces entirely by hand. Through the years, M.P. Davis art deco style creations have become highly collectible.

How satisfying it would be for me to dare dream that I had a hand in the making of a now-antique piece that someone today has paid thousands of pounds to acquire. Alas, however, as a whelp and newbie, I was initially assigned to perform 'scut work' for a few shillings per week: running errands, gathering and disposing of refuse, and other menial, often unsavory tasks.

First thing in the morning, I was tasked with collecting from glue-pots the thick, noxious residues of the prior day's labors. Then, with abundant elbow-grease, I had to muscle water into the obstinate sludge until it achieved a uniformly pliable consistency. Next, I would apply the reconstituted blend by brush to wood veneers, saturating them, before clamping them together so that they could bond for twenty-four hours and be ready for the crafters the following day.

Such labors did not constitute an apprenticeship in the craft of woodworking. What I didn't learn through hands-on experience, however, I did manage to pick up through patient, attentive observation – a practice that would pay dividends again and again.

The times were such that most businesses economized on local and not-too-distant deliveries through the use of public transportation trams, also known as trolley cars. If, during the course of a day's production, it was determined that iron bedframe units were needed, the low-man-on-the-totem pole 'apprentice' would be dispatched to fetch and return with them, regardless of the total weight of the load. Though the ironmonger's hardware store was situated conveniently about five minutes ride time from the shop, wrangling the load and bearing it for the pedestrian portions of the errand often proved to be an arduous undertaking.

Englanders of every stripe and position in the caste system pecking order revere their tea breaks. Whether at the morning break, lunchtime, or four o'clock tea, it was always "*Sidney*-this" and "*Sidney*-that." Collect and rinse the beverage mugs. Take everyone's special orders. Biscuits. Buns. Pasties. Pie. And Coconut Tart – portions of which, given the lack of refrigeration, often appeared to have been predigested by the local bakery's contingent of determined flies.

Even the building's lift didn't miss an opportunity to challenge the aspiring novitiate. The manually operated device was self-propelled via its rope-and-pulley mechanics. In hindsight, no modern day fitness center apparatus could hope to emulate the stubborn resistance of that rudimentary contraption.

I would return home exhausted, filthy, and a sight to behold.

20

Somewhat degraded and discouraged, looking at times as though I had just emerged from the pit of a coal mine, I was miserable. I felt as if I were being milked and bilked as cheap child labor, which doubtless I was.

One day, my materials supply assignment entailed bearing two considerable loads simultaneously from the hardware store: the usual batch of bedframes, which I balanced on my shoulders, plus a cardboard box of metal 'domes,' which I struggled to keep tucked under one arm. The domes were substantial finials of a sort nailed to the wooden feet of table and chair legs by the cabinetmakers.

On the way back, as muscular control suddenly flagged, I lost my grip on the box. It burst open as soon as it struck the pavement, spewing a gross of shiny metal domes into the middle of the roadway. I laid down the ironwork at once and scooped up as many of the scattered and scraped domes as I could, tucking them into apron pockets. Eventually I was able to make it back to the M.P. Davis shop, where I shambled in, hunched over, my neck and head straining against the apron-tugging gravity of the better part of one hundred forty-four mini-cannonballs.

That was it. I'd had enough of exploitation and ignominy. I quit.

Once again, with mild chagrin, I returned to see my placement counselor. What was to be my next job? My sisters, praise be, came up with a brilliant idea. How about our Sidney becoming a *genuine* tailor—a fashion designer and pattern maker? It all sounded very pie-in-the-sky, beyond the reach of a virtually unschooled lad unsure of himself in hardscrabble times.

But what choices did I have? Not many, I am afraid – or so I was given to understand. Once more, therefore, I found myself under long-term contract, as an apprentice to Mr. Rosenberg, whose boutique basic dry goods operation consisted of one tailor and one machinist. My boss did all the cutting, which I soon learned was from the identical set of patterns each season, with little or no tangible variation. Their process and products, being at the cheaper end of the trade, were anything but 'bespoke.'

21

"So much for pie-in-the-sky. Sidney," I said to myself. "Here I am again, grist for the mill." I'd become virtually indentured through the fine print in a small font contract I couldn't possibly hope to read, much less understand. Opportunities for acquiring the skills to advance ran the gamut from nil to never.

Soon after I started working for Rosenberg Tailors, they moved into a new building on Commercial Road, very close to where I was born. Now I was given my daily routine orders, which were to answer the telephone (still a newly commercialized convenience), polish the showroom floor, and keep the offices clean.

Not once, ever, had I answered a telephone. None of the families we knew had such an exotic appliance in their residence. The very first day I started work, when I was busy tidying up the showroom, the mute box on the wall behind me suddenly rang with the clarion insistence of a ringside bell in a prizefight. My heart leapt to my throat, and I nearly jumped out of my skin.

I can see it now. With a deep breath, I gathered my wits, picked the receiver up off the hook, put it to my ear, and called out, "Hullo," not knowing what to expect or what to do next. The caller was similarly befuddled. He himself either didn't know how to speak into his newfangled gizmo, or he was hard of hearing – or he was so incensed with my shouting into my end of the phone that he responded in kind, bellowing and nearly bursting my eardrum. My instant reaction was to drop the earpiece as if it had scorched my hand and withdraw, leaving it dangling from the wire, swaying uselessly like a dislocated limb.

In short order, common sense and a lick of courage enabled me to retrieve the squawking knob and hastily return it, with an all too audible *kee-lack*, to its cradle. I had hung up, terminating the episode. Then I looked left and right and over my shoulder to see if anyone had caught sight of me being terrorized by Alexander Graham Bell's invention. No. I was in luck. *Phew!*

When not sweeping and polishing the showroom floor, or performing other tidying-up chores, I served as the shop's gofer – picking up food and drink for tea and lunch breaks as before, bringing back raw materials from one of the local trimmings stores, and delivering final products to customers.

More through experimentation than formal training, I did become rather expert at packing heavy coats into cardboard boxes, which I was then tasked with delivering, via London public transport, to our retail store customers. Mounting and alighting from trolley cars whilst wrangling the awkwardly proportioned cartons was forever a hassle. First, they had to be loaded up front just so with the driver; then I had to run to the rear of the vehicle and leap onto the boarding platform before the trolley lurched forward to resume plying its route. On reaching the relevant stop, I had to execute the reverse maneuver – and ever so swiftly at that, lest the driver exert his authority capriciously and take off with the goods still on board.

I made it my business to learn and master the basics. Practicing sewing with needle, thimble, and cotton thread, I would sit cross-legged on the table, bent over, clenching the neck of the needle between thumb and forefinger of the right hand as I worked it into a piece of scrap cloth held in the left. Between the intensity of the effort and the associated muscular discomfort, I found the repetitive process to be somewhat dizzying and nauseating. Nevertheless, I persevered. Regardless of my age, experience, education, and station in life, I was not going to allow a needle and thread to get the better of me.

In due course, I became expert in sewing fast and well. But no sooner had that bar been cleared than boredom and restlessness set in. I needed to be challenged. I wanted more. Always more. More knowledge, more training, more trust, greater reward, more out of life.

Repeatedly I would complain to my boss and to my counselor that Mr. Rosenberg wasn't living up to his end of our contract; he wasn't teaching me the trade. Mr. Rosenberg, set in his ways and needing only unskilled labor to complement the compact crew of his boutique operation, sought to placate me with a sop: a few extra pence in the weekly pay packet.

What was I to do? The baseline fact of the matter was that my counselor was so overloaded with the case files of delinquent youth finishing school and pouring into the 'labor force' each year, he couldn't possibly hope to keep track of his charges and help them to make fundamental course corrections, much less help them to realize and maximize their true potential.

There's a part of me that wants to believe the *Jewish Board of Guardians* had good intentions when placing young teens into industrial occupations. They were supposed to be able to work their way up the ladder as they learned a trade, from apprentice to journeyman and eventually to master craftsman, much the way it had been for centuries, rooted in the medieval guild system.

That was a promise, however, destined not to be kept. With a country-wide double-digit unemployment rate and a tide of school-leaving juveniles entering the labor pool each and every year, employers had the upper hand and used it to their advantage. One system that did seem to function well despite the disadvantageous times was that of unabashed, naked nepotism. Family-owned businesses took care of family members, first and foremost, often without regard to motivation, talent, or ultimate contribution to the bottom line.

Failure to live up to the letter and spirit of the contract was one thing. That was injury. Discrimination based on blood line – that was both injury and intolerably unjust insult. I was not bitter, mind you. I was realistic, resigned to the then-prevalent facts of life.

After having sought alternative employment for some period of time, yet with no new job prospects on the horizon, I made peace with those facts of life and quit. For the first time in recorded history, the name *Sidney Fersht* was entered in the official registry of those on the dole.


## Becoming Streetwise

All I could really do to distinguish myself from a legion of other post-pubescent job seekers was to sew by hand speedily and with proficiency. I certainly wasn't sufficiently qualified to gain work as a tailor. Furthermore, the rag trade, as it was known, was highly seasonal. Garment manufacturers hired freely at the outset and fired with equal abandon at the culmination, shoving the drones out of the hive.

I took advantage of each such experience, migrating from shop to shop, factory to factory, learning more each time, honing my craft as best I could. Seasons came and went with unremarkable regularity as the calendar pages flipped from one year to the next. By the time I had reached the age of seventeen, I was earning what was then considered a married man's wages – but only for the duration of the several-months-long season before being laid off.

How well I remember those years of grinding, self-directed apprenticeship. The stench of coal fire smokestack emissions thick in the air as I made rounds through the industrial areas. The winters unrelentingly damp and chilling to the bone. Underheated, if at all, factory buildings, some hailing from the late 19th century. I had zero body fat – still don't to this day. For temporary relief as I labored in the drafty expanses of the factory floor, I would warm two pressing irons on the gas jets used to prep them for purpose and then stand directly on top of them, all the while expressing hot breath onto my fingertips to maintain circulation and sense of touch. If my digits stiffened in the least, they wouldn't be sufficiently nimble to enable me to perform my tasks. Resourcefulness. Pluck. Determination. Such are the attributes one must muster in order to survive in a milieu redolent of *Oliver Twist.*

Lightyears before such terms as 'carpal tunnel syndrome' or 'repetitive stress injury' came into vogue, I strained the overtaxed muscles of my right hand, causing the connective tissues of wrist and lower forearm to swell up with fluid and render me incapable of performing my duties.

A visit to the doctor resulted in immobilization of my right arm in a plaster cast running from wrist to armpit, precluding any exertion of the musculature of the hand. For several months I was out of commission and most unhappily back on the dole. I was reminded of my father's similarly forced period of convalescence and inactivity. Dark thoughts began to creep in. Was this to be my destiny? To be a knockabout semi-casual laborer the rest of my life? To suffer the slings and arrows of ill fortune in a physically demanding, depersonalized environment?

Fortunately, it was not in my nature to dwell in the morose swamps of self-doubt and self-pity. My destiny was *mine* to make, no one else's. I soldiered on. I once again found gainful employment, this time with the prestigious house of Ellis and Goldstein, one of the East End's premier makers of high end womenswear.

Yes, the days were long and the work repetitive, but I was pulling my own weight and earning a decent wage, albeit ever with one eye on the fashion season calendar in anticipation of the predictable pink slip at season's end. Except this time, *mirabile dictu*, the foreman had taken notice of the disciplined, stalwart lad who gave it his all and never gave up on himself. He kept me on. I – the once-upon-a-time shy, fearful eighth grade graduate – had risen above my station. I began feeling better about myself and my prospects. For the first time, I ventured to indulge in a sense of job security.

Concurrently, rapidly mounting geopolitical tensions fueled by Germany's militarism and acts of territorial expansion seemed to be ameliorated through Prime Minister Neville Chamberlain's deft diplomacy. On October 1, 1938, he returned to London from a meeting convened with *Reichskanzler* Adolf Hitler in Munich, having achieved the evening before a *modus vivendi* with him – an agreement 'symbolic of the desire of our two peoples never to go to war with one another again.' At home, Chamberlain was fêted as a hero.

Good news all 'round. The seventeen-year-old of 1938 persevered, prospered, and became the eighteen-year-old of 1939. Perhaps, I ventured optimistically, things will continue to become more reliably stable for me and my loved ones.

Then, on September 1, 1939, having mocked and derided the Munich agreement as a 'scrap of paper,' Hitler directed his *Wehrmacht* to attack and invade Poland. World War II on the

European continent had, by that act and other aggressions, commenced with fury.

# CHAPTER 3
# WAR

Great Britain was vastly unprepared for the shooting war that had been thrust upon us. Winston Churchill, First Lord of the Admiralty for the second time in his illustrious service to country, became the new prime minister on May 10, 1940. Three days later, addressing his cabinet, and later the House of Commons, he delivered a sobering dose of straight-talk that steeled the country for what lay ahead: "I have nothing to offer but blood, toil, tears and sweat." At every critical juncture in the fight to preserve our way of life and conquer the wicked foe, Churchill sustained and invigorated us, mobilizing the English language, rousing our embattled island nation to action, inspiring courage and unyielding resolve. In our darkest hour, he shone a light.

To use a familiar branch of service term, the country closed ranks, galvanized by Churchill's no-nonsense, proudly defiant rhetoric. My brother-in-law Victor, a World War I veteran deemed too agèd for combat, became instead a civil defense Volunteer Warden, later to be promoted to Chief Warden of our district. His duties, like those of others commissioned to serve aboveground whilst the general population sought refuge in shelters, put him in harm's way:

During World War II, whilst London underwent constant bombardment from the Luftwaffe, the capital's Air Raid Wardens went above and beyond the call of duty to serve the British people. Not only did they patrol the streets during the Blackout, learn first aid techniques and risk their lives on a regular basis as unpaid volunteers, they also undertook the task of boosting morale during the dark times of the War.[9]

## The Battle of Britain

British novelist William Samson called it 'one of the fairest days of the century – a day of clear warm air and high blue skies.' On Saturday, September 7, 1940, shortly after 4 p.m., the first wave of *Messerschmitt* fighter aircraft and their protected contingent of heavy bombers breached the airspace over the coast of southern England. The *Blitz*, as it would be dubbed by the British press, had begun, showering death and ruin across broad swaths of a land soon to be fighting for its way of life and very survival.

Our district's Air Raid Warden HQ command post was a belowground bunker at the streetcorner. One entered through a manhole and descended an iron stairway into a compact eight-by-seven-foot tomb-like space furnished minimally with worktable, two folding chairs, and a rudimentary, hand-crank, magneto-powered telephone set.

In short order, Victor recruited me to serve as a volunteer warden. My first assignment, motoring on bicycle and walking door-to-door, was to map the location of hydrants and to perform a basic headcount census of residential dwellings – number of occupants, ages, and genders. Why? Having suffered Germany's perfidious use of chemical weaponry in the first world war, Britain was preparing to distribute gas masks to its citizenry.

At the conclusion of each day's fact-finding tour, I'd prepare a written report, making carbon copies for distribution up the line. As the Cockney would say, 'I did my bit.'

Even before the onset of war, assembly-ready *Anderson* bomb shelters[10] had been developed and delivered to those homes which

---

[9] 'The Dual Role of Air Raid Wardens,' Tabatha Parker, *West End at War* (March 22, 2011), http://www.westendatwar.org.uk/page_id__175.aspx.

[10] 'In 1938, with the outbreak of World War II on the horizon, Sir John Anderson [Lord Privy Seal under Neville Chamberlain] was placed in charge of air-raid preparations in Britain. He commissioned engineers to design a cheap

featured sufficient outdoor space to accommodate them. The kits consisted of curved, corrugated metal sheets that one bolted together to form a protective shell and canopy. Municipal crews excavated the plot, much as gravediggers preparing a burial vault, to a depth of four feet. The completed structure, measuring a standard 6 feet tall by 6.5 long by 4.5 wide, stuck out aboveground by a height of two feet.

After that the owners could do with them as they pleased. It was necessary to bank as much earth as possible over the sides of the metal sheets for protection. Some people put wooden floors inside, with benches to sleep on. Many beautified the shelters by growing flowers over and around. The main purpose was to protect occupants from high-velocity shrapnel; it certainly would not stand up to a direct or nearby hit.

During sustained periods of bombardment, families occupied their shelters for nights on end, learning to tolerate the confines of the primitive accommodation with venerable British stiff upper lip *sangfroid*. Acceptance of stark realities and exigencies borne of necessity—that aforementioned mother of invention – knew no bounds.

Running to the shelter became a nightly routine. The sirens blared their warnings with the setting of the sun. You could set your clock by the roaring engines of squadron after squadron of German bombers menacing overhead. If you heard the mounting crescendo of a *whooshing* sound, your gut tightened. You knew a plunging bomb was close at hand. Then you waited with rampant

---

and simple shelter which could be distributed to the population. [Measuring] six feet tall, 6.5 feet long, and 4.5 feet wide, the corrugated metal shelters were a snug fit for a family of six. They were buried four feet under owners' yards, their arched roofs covered with a layer of soil. The shelters were distributed for free to poorer residents. Wealthier residents could purchase one for a small fee. Many chose to incorporate the shelters into their gardens, planting vegetables and flowers on top of them. Residents even held competitions for prettiest shelter. By the time the Blitz began, over 2 million Anderson shelters had been erected.' Source: *1939 – 1944: Backyard bunkers of the Blitz.* Alex Q. Arbuckle: https://mashable.com/2015/07/24/wwii-backyard-bunkers/#uTV486RgmZqQ.

anxiety for the explosion, praying that it would detonate somewhere else, anywhere else – but also by some miracle of fate or hand of providence bring no harm to others.

Next you heard the shrill klaxon horns of auxiliary ambulances and fire brigades speeding toward the trauma sites to battle the conflagrations, rescue and tend to the wounded, gather the dead, examine structures to determine their viability, and exert every effort to save lives, calm nerves, and preserve order.

In the morning, when the all-clear had sounded, you exited your shelter, having had light and fitful sleep, cleaned up quickly, and prepared for another workday. That evening, the cycle repeated. The sapping anxiety inherent in night after night of seemingly random bombardment lay in not knowing if or when your number might be up. Beginning on September 7, 1940, Bosch ordnance rained hell on London for 56 out of 57 nights and days.

Shockingly close to home, on a moonless Sunday evening five weeks into the campaign, a complex of apartments and retail shops sustained a direct aerial torpedo hit, leveling the structure and either burning, suffocating, or drowning – from burst water mains – scores upon scores of occupants, plus those who had sought refuge in subterranean shelters. For several days, recovery teams extracted bodies, covered in tarpaulin sheets, in a grim processional of "There But for the Grace of God Go I."

Firefighters, ambulance teams, constabulary personnel, air raid wardens, sanitation crews, and volunteers of all stripes worked dusk to dawn to deal with the aftermath of the nightly raids. The morning after, as I made rounds on bicycle within the district, I encountered the shockingly sad and bizarre still life tableaux of the war zone. Commercial establishments reduced to rubble. Gaping moonscape craters. Houses that had taken a direct hit, one of them with nothing left except a portion of a parlor wall adorned with a solitary figurine resting on a mantel shelf over the fireplace. Apartment buildings stripped of an exterior wall, their units exposed to the elements, as if a life-size dollhouse in complete disarray had been plopped down in the middle of a rubble-strewn wasteland.

One morning, having pedaled to my place of employment, I remained astride my bicycle, staring dumbfounded in disbelief. The building had disappeared. In its stead, a massive pile of bricks, timber, shattered glass, and twisted metal. It, too, had taken a direct hit.

I didn't know what to do. I poked about the rubble to see if I could salvage something, anything to help. Little of any meaningful use had survived the blast. Of all things, however, I did manage to extricate from the wreckage, uncannily unharmed, *well, hullo, there!* My very own first pair of twelve-inch fabric shears.

Despite having had their livelihoods obliterated in the blink of an eye, the owners of Ellis and Goldstein stood tall, remitting accrued wages to their employees. Honor and duty, regardless of adversity. Such spine.

I've kept those defiant shears ever since as a memento of sorts, as a symbol of the kind of stouthearted spirit that enabled us as a people to rise above rubble and ruin, and carry on.


## First Allegiance

How best to carry on? Whether I asked that question of myself 'out loud' or harkened to an inner voice of conscience demanding to be heard, who knows? What I do know is that I answered the question and the call as best I could. In my twentieth year, with Britain under siege, I made my way to the nearest *Combined Recruitment Centre* and joined the Royal Air Force.

Celia, my big sister and dearly protective mother figure, was none too happy to see her youngest sibling about to be caught up in the machinery of war. Nevertheless, she understood. I was of age, and it was the honorable thing to do.

The armed services wasted no time in calling enlistees to report to duty. Straightaway, I was issued a railway ticket to an RAF boot camp in Arbroath, Scotland, high up on the North Sea-facing east coast, northeast of Edinburgh and Dundee.

Far, far away from the wrenching travails of a hometown

being pummeled on a daily basis, the quaint fishing village of Arbroath – also known as Aberbrothock – should have offered respite and repose. But for those such as I, newly uniformed, there were to be no quiet mornings spent angling in a brook or dockside off the pier. No ale-soaked lunches with the mates, swapping tall tales down at the pub. No long, leisurely ambles along narrow cobblestone lanes, popping in and out of shops here and there, admiring the townspeople's daughters in their crisp cotton smocks as they helped out in the family dry goods store or fresh produce stalls on the marketplace common.

None of that. Only boot camp. Six weeks of living hell.

The training was relentless. It demanded every ounce of effort and will, punishing the body until the body became steel and the mind its equal. It made a man of me.

One of our first orders was to report to sick bay to receive tetanus shots plus three others in the same arm at the same time. I became so sick my head was spinning. My left arm swelled and became fairly rigid, and the rest of my body ached all over. As we'd been given the weekend off, I spent it in bed – not in a barracks, mind you, but in a private home.

Because of overcrowding at the base, some of us had been 'boarded out.' Our landlady, a Mrs. Alva MacDougall, and her two teenage children were wonderfully considerate, simple, churchgoing folk. Having billeted other entry-level servicemen before, Mrs. MacDougall was well aware of the rough time we'd been having so very far away from kith and kin.

On that particular weekend, as I and others convalesced in our rooms, she prepared meals for us and had them sent up. Famished, I partook – for the first time in my life – of meat banned by *Leviticus* and *Deuteronomy*: a cloven-footed, non-cud-chewing, and therefore abhorrently non-kosher animal. Swine. Pig, to be exact, sectioned and prepared across a spectrum of its classic manifestations: rashers of hickory smoked bacon, thick slabs of gammon, and plump, seasoned sausage. Farm-raised and cured.

Salty. Savory. Sinfully delicious. *Thank you*, Mrs. MacDougall!

One morning, as I sat outside on the grass, alternatively polishing my boots and the brass buttons on my cadet jacket, the industrious Mrs. MacDougall came by, snatched the boots off the ground, and harrumphed, "That will never do, young man. Follow me." Off we marched, straight into the kitchen. "Sit down right there," she commanded, indicating one of the side chairs. Then, having spread sheets of newspaper on the table, she commenced to shining my boots herself. Her labors completed, she declared with a smile of immense satisfaction, "There. That's better now isn't it!" I reciprocated, thanking her. She nodded, half-turned to leave, and then explained, "You're about to risk your life for our country, Sidney. I want you to feel comfortable during your short stay here." And off she went, the most amiable, considerate, generous drill instructor I would ever have the pleasure of knowing.

The brass at the Arbroath boot camp, however, had a wholly different perspective on what it meant to be a DI – a drill instructor. Monday morning at 5.00 a.m. sharp, as civilians slept and arboreal creatures of nearby wooded areas skittered and squawked on being rudely awakened, we were marched to open fields to conduct rigorous body-building exercises. We had not fully recovered from post-inoculation soreness. Groans and moans fell on deaf ears. Our tormentors were instilling obedience and building endurance. "Pain is good. Get used to it."

There was no Mum or Dad to run home to. No turning back. They owned us, and we belonged to them. In our short stay, they used every means available to prepare us for what lay ahead. *They knew*. We didn't. Physical prowess was but one of their missions. Stripping us of individuality, self-interest, and emotional immaturity – that was paramount. They trained us to perform as a unit, as a team. The DIs, bless their iron-willed hearts, seemed to be in competition with one another as to who would turn out the most disciplined and effective squad when put through our paces on the Holy of Holies, the parade ground.

We couldn't appreciate it fully at the time, of course, but doubtless their stern, uncompromising dedication to mission saved lives.

Grudgingly at first, then more willingly, we responded to the regimen. Reveille at 5 a.m. Hustle to the parade ground, regardless of weather conditions. Strenuous conditioning exercises, always with a higher stretch goal – no pun intended – to test and expand our limits. A four-mile run to the village and back. March to the showers, dress for the day, then – and only then – a hasty mess hall breakfast, hastened by the men with stripes: "Arses up! This 'ere ain't no picnic."

Next, weaponry. Stripping, cleaning, and reassembling the rifle. Sighting and marksmanship on the firing range. Fieldcraft. Handling grenades. Running assault courses under live machinegun fire. (Yes, there were casualties.) Protocols and equipment for dealing with chemical warfare.

Further rounds of marching and close formation drills, hours on end, day after day, until the squad's DI was satisfied that the unit responded as one to his command. And then more of the same until it became second nature. *Team, team, team.*

Even the so-called little things were big things. Learning when and how one must salute commissioned officers proved to be enormously important. We spent countless hours on parade being instructed: one-two-three *up!* … then *snap!* the shortest way down. Encountering or passing an officer without saluting was considered to be and treated as a punishable offense. We became reasonably paranoid – to the extent that rather than risk committing a crime of omission, we snapped to and saluted just about anything in uniform, including the base civilian milkman.

Barracks inspections, though not as fraught with fear of infraction as that of officer recognition, preyed nevertheless on our nerves. An instructional poster mounted on an inside wall provided visual confirmation of how a perfectly kept barracks should look. Pillows and folded blankets positioned just so. One's kit gear displayed ever so neatly at the foot of the bed so that its contents could be inspected with ease and speed to identify deficiencies or to seize contraband.

We stood at attention, forming a crisp row, in the exact bedside position indicated by the illustrative poster. The squadron sergeant, wearing white gloves and trailed down the central aisle by his subordinate corporal, paused at each airman's station, betraying nothing in his demeanor to indicate either satisfaction or the lack thereof – unless and until he came to an abrupt halt to comment on a cadet's bearing or uniform, or to poke around in the fellow's kit array as the trainee's guts tightened with apprehension. *Did I miss something? Did I do something wrong? What's he gonna do?*

## Religion on Parade

Sometimes religion isn't about service to one's chosen supreme everlasting being. Sometimes it's about serving to facilitate the consummation of mortal man's immediate lust. Henry VIII, in order to divorce Catherine of Aragon and marry Anne Boleyn, broke with the Catholic Church in 1534, thereby establishing the supremacy of the Church of England.

Thereafter, the Anglican Church paid no allegiance to the Vatican. Sundays, however, were ever sacrosanct, to be observed religiously. And in that regard, the British military high command enforced strict compliance. For the brass, Sunday church parades were special occasions requiring attendance by all able-bodied airmen, regardless of one's chosen faith. We were to look our best: clean-shaven; uniform spotless, with sharp creases down the trouser legs; boots shined to a mirror-like finish; body attitude upright and respectful. To participate in the Sunday spectacle on hallowed parade ground was considered to be a high honor after a mere three weeks of basic training.

I can see it now. Our legion of newbies marched to the field and arrayed in perfectly formed squadrons, three to an aviation 'wing.' The Chief Warrant Officer, the highest of NCOs, ceremoniously handed the assembled groups over to the Wing Commander, who presided from the dais, the raised platform from which the assembled clergy and he would conduct the ritual service and military musical accompaniment.

The event, clearly, was one of inclusion. We were together as one in service to country. There was something noble and transcendent in the moment. My heart filled with pride. *Sidney Fersht*, I said to myself, *you…"* My reverie was interrupted by the stentorian voice of the Wing Commander: "All Jews and others not of the faith fall out and face the brick wall."

As Mrs. MacDougall acknowledged in her pure kindheartedness and Christian charity, I, along with my mates, we were all putting our lives on the line for the cause. And yet, despite that supreme equality, we were being singled out, forced from the ranks undeservèdly, and made to feel like pariahs. I was thoroughly crushed and humiliated.

The irony would grow on me later, the irony that a country waging war against Nazi Germany, a state ruled by a sociopath and his cadre of criminally complicit sadists, a fascist state that had industrialized genocide – the very fact that my own country would itself countenance the practice of a form of religious persecution was anathema.

"All Jews and others…" That was the first time I'd come face-to-face with the specter of such blatant discrimination in the military, but it would not be the last. Far from it. More than once during my five-and-a-half years of service, as I proceeded from post to post, from campaign to campaign, I had cause to reflect and wonder why, with our bodies exposed to enemy fire, must we suffer the threat of an insidious enemy within our own ranks: the dagger of anti-Semitism.

## First Postings

Six weeks. Forty-two days of boot camp. Roughly one one-thousandth of my life to date, yet then it seemed a lifetime. Without a doubt, it was a pivotal chapter of maturation and a telling turning point. The passing-out parade, as it is called, was a line of demarcation. The raw recruit has been molded and sculpted into a fighting machine. Graduation here was prelude not to career in commerce or to further academic studies, but rather to learning

37

more of the business of war.

Before entering the parade ground to commence the program of pomp and glory, each airman had to undergo a close physical inspection to ensure sharpness of appearance and perfection in the presentation of uniform. Military precision had to be achieved whether standing stock still or in the execution of our choreographed movements. The band played triumphant marching music. The Station Commander, a thin smile creasing the craggy expanse of his leathery, battle-worn puss, took and returned the salutes offered by man after man on their way to who knew where.

Our rite of passage complete, we were issued orders to new postings, some to acquire knowledge and experience in trades and specialties instrumental in killing the enemy, others directly to forward positions where they, too, would become further immersed in the art and science of achieving payback and conquering the Axis powers. I examined my orders and travel warrants: three hundred seventeen kilometers southeast to Yorkshire's RAF Station Driffield.

Unhappily, I was detailed to serve at the associated bomb dump in nearby Southburn. Perhaps, given my dismal elementary school record, they thought such mindless grunt work was all I was good for. I rued not having made my tailoring aptitudes known. Had I done so, I might have been posted to the Quartermaster's corps, altering uniforms, sewing on chevron patches , anything to leverage my talents and dexterity with textiles whilst keeping these vocational skills sharp for life after service. *But no, Sidney: orders are orders. The bomb dump it is.*

Being uncomfortably within range of the *Luftwaffe*, the facility, known as an *Air Ammunition Park,* was concealed in a forested patch accessible via the Southburn railway station, the perimeter surrounded by barbed-wire fencing. On entering the main gate, I was challenged by the on-guard sentry. In due course, I was be given such sedentary duty myself. Bombs weighing up to five hundred pounds apiece were freighted directly into our camp via a railway spur. They were ever so carefully and deftly offloaded by crane and stacked on 'sleepers' set in cushioning beds of cinders. Their detonators, potentially volatile explosive devices essential to making the bombs go *boom*, were stored in heavily fortified shed-bunkers camouflaged by earthen berms and unremarkable indigenous shrubbery.

We were on call twenty-four seven, a hop-skip-and-a-jump from the Driffield base, to feed the monsters: formidably dark, looming twin engine *Vickers Wellington* long-range bombers.

We on the ground had immense respect and admiration for the courageous, spirited men who crewed them. They were members of an exclusive club – *The Few* – so named by Winston Churchill in his address to the House of Commons, as he paid homage:

> The gratitude of every home in our Island, in our Empire, and indeed throughout the world … goes out to the British airmen who, undaunted by odds, unwearied in their constant challenge and mortal danger, are turning the tide of the world war by their prowess and by their devotion. Never in the field of human conflict was so much owed by so many to so few. All hearts go out to the fighter pilots, whose brilliant actions we see with our own eyes day after day; but we must never forget that all the time, night after night, month after month, our bomber squadrons travel far into Germany, find their targets in the darkness by the highest navigational skill, aim their attacks, often under the heaviest fire, often with serious loss.[11]

More than once, RAF Driffield suffered such sacrifice. The morning after a sortie, when empty spaces on the airfield gave stark evidence of the failure of crews to return safely, hearts were most grievously heavy. We bore the gloom and sadness with brave faces, knowing that those who perished or were taken captive would expect us to honor their devotion by carrying on. Always, carry on.

---

[11] August 20, 1940.

## Unfriendly Skies

We had little doubt that the *Luftwaffe* high command was well aware of our actual location. Precision bombing, however, was another matter entirely. Nevertheless, German pilots and navigational crew, supplied with maps and aerial photographs, were able to follow railway tracks to reach target areas and release their payloads.

Fortunately for us, with the profusion of small towns and villages dotted throughout the sprawling farmlands of Yorkshire, railway depots surrounding our enclave were by-and-large indistinguishable one from the other. As the Jerry bombardiers commanded *Bomben los!*, the result was often a seemingly scattershot affair, albeit with some missiles striking home. The sky around us would be ablaze with incendiaries, many of them igniting fires on our patch. We had neither the time nor inclination to worry about our mortal danger as we scurried to drown the flames licking at the perimeter of storage vaults housing highly explosive fuses and detonators. If something bad were to happen, we'd never know it.

Aboveground water tanks served as gravity-fed fire-fighting hydrants. That was virtually their sole purpose. Nonetheless, boys will be boys – especially drunken ones. I can see it now. Christmastime. Bitterly cold, with a nasty subzero wind chill. One of our band, a beefy, boisterously inebriated Irishman, decided it was time for a swim – in the emergency water supply. First, the bear of a man had to scale and enter the cistern, then chop a hole in the thick crust of ice that had formed atop the reservoir. That alone should have deterred his alcohol-fueled escapade. But no, he dove in, naked as a blooming jaybird. An instantly excruciating experience ensued. He yawped for help and struggled wildly and ineffectually to escape the brutal effects of near-freezing liquid assaulting warm flesh. It took several of us to fish the poor sod out.

## Food Glorious Food

One of the benefits of routine is predictability. Two of the curses are boredom and endless boredom. With regularity, I'd apply for transfer to another, more challenging post where my duties – hopefully – would be commensurate with my skills. With equal regularity, my request form, lacking the CO's signature of approval, would come back marked "DENIED."

Guard duties, though being the pinnacle of tedium, did offer one potential salutary feature. If I could finagle being assigned to the early morning shift, before the mess hall boys showed up to man the kitchen, I could cook my own breakfast. And that I did. Nothing like starting the day with a lavish serving of a half dozen eggs and a matching number of rashers of thick country bacon to cheer mind and belly.

Being able to slake one's appetite in such a way was a luxury, one of the very few available to us working stiffs in uniform. Foodstuffs – calories, more to the point – are as vital as materiel in the conduct of warfare. Rationing amongst the civilian population is a necessary adjunct, if not a prerequisite, to sustaining the armed forces.

That said, the reality is that within the ranks, there was a pecking order. A breakfast of high protein, savory bacon-and-eggs – a commonplace meal during peacetime – was a highly prized commodity. Our cooks, knowing which side their bread was buttered on, would schedule the treats for the weekend menu when most of the enlisted men were on pass. Ergo, more for the brass and NCOs. Ergo, my periodic and probably all too transparent ploy: "Sergeant, I'm happy to do my bit and volunteer first shift at the gatehouse tomorrow." *Thank you very much.*

### First Furlough

Being granted leave entitled one to a railway warrant which defrayed a modest portion of the expense of travel. With meager pay and severely limited financial resources, most of us had to learn to beat the system in order to travel long distances to reach the bosom of hearth and home. We had a go-to technique – and please, don't call it a crime or even so much as petty theft.

Remember, we were men at war, serving our country on the front lines, or soon to be. We merited our small acts of convenience. After all, in lifting our spirits, they served the cause. Where was I? Yes, our go-to technique – how clever we were! The day before our intended trip, we'd purchase a cheap one-way ticket from Southburn to Bainton, the next stop on the Selby-Driffield railway line. With clever use of erasure, chemicals, and matching ink, we'd eliminate Bainton and insert our ultimate destination – in my case, Kings Cross, London, via Leicester.

Alas, too many servicemen ran the same game. The authorities soon caught on and began policing the practice to the extent that one day I was nabbed at the terminal's exit gate by a railway copper who put my feet to the fire. "Sir," he said, "come with me." I floated some cock- and-bull story about being strapped, needing to get home to an ailing parent, and foolishly buying it off another fellow. I offered to pony up the fare if only he'd let me go. He did. My short-lived career as a ticket-fixer, I vowed, was over.

And thus came a time when, genuinely short of cash and needing to return to base, I put my thumb out to hitchhike. Eventually, a good bloke driving an open bed cement truck stopped and invited me to ride in the back – which I did, all the way to Leicester, a driving distance of about one hundred sixty kilometers.

By the time he dropped me off, my RAF blues, along with the rest of me, had become caked in a crust of ashen grey dust from head to toe. I must have looked like a ghostly apparition to circumspect pedestrians who prudently stepped aside as I threaded my way to the center of town to avail myself of the public loo facilities. An attendant, sensitive to my plight, brushed me down, removing layer after layer of the toxic grit from my face and body.

Why did we go to such lengths to spend time with family? Need we ask? No inconvenience or ignominy of travel could hope to deter us. Familiar faces, loving hugs, home-cooked meals, sleeping late, being treated as a hero – how glorious and uplifting, indeed.

## "Arrest and Trial"

Though my days as an amateur forger had been put to a stop, I was not immune to committing sheer acts of stupidity.

Within the span of the five-and-a-half years that I spent in service to flag and country, I was charged only once with an infraction, but it was a most serious one, an unwitting negligent act which might very well have put me and others at risk.

One day at the Driffield air base, as I toiled away within the confines of an empty hangar, Flight Lieutenant Harris, a strapping fellow whose family ran a pork processing plant, happened in and immediately took me to task. "Airman Fersht, what the bloody hell are you doing smoking a cigarette in here?!" The air was thick with the odor of aviation petrol. Any fool, but apparently not this one, should have had the common sense not to light up within the confines of such a potentially volatile atmosphere. "Consider yourself under Open Arrest," he continued, snatching the offending butt from my hand and extinguishing it under heel of boot.

Open Arrest entails reporting to the guard house immediately. I can picture it now. Chastened and shaken, I mounted a bicycle and reported to the guardhouse, where I was directed to sign the register of non-incarcerated offenders. That task was to be repeated every waking hour until lights out, day after day, until I received the order to appear before the Station Commanding Officer to answer the charges made against me.

I was appalled to think what might happen because of my inherently reckless decision to light up in the wrong place at the wrong time. My mind was racing. *Nothing happened*, I say to myself, *but still I'm in Dutch for doing it, nonetheless*.

As luck would have it, even though I had been in uniform for only a few months, somewhere along the line, I remembered, there was that chance conversation with Sergeant Christopher Russell, a longtime regular army NCO. For whatever reason, he had waxed forth on the topic of rules, regulations, and the military police. Anything from fisticuffs in the pub to an afternoon AWOL walkabout could land someone in the brig. Sergeant Russell stuck out his chest with pride, flashed a conspiratorial wink, and boasted, "There isn't a charge in the service you can't wriggle out of if you keep your wits about you. Look at the way the charge is written. Look for an angle. Words matter. If they don't get it right, exactly right, there's your escape hatch."

The morning of reckoning came. Proceedings were performed with military formality and regimented precision. The overall impression was that of court-martial. I was not the only one on the docket. We were a sorry bunch, standing ramrod straight at attention, waiting our respective turns on the griddle. Mine came. A gravelly voice commanded, "Fersht, Sidney – fall out and come with me." I was marched into the CO's office and ordered to halt short of his desk. Dizzy with apprehension, I had managed to preserve the presence of mind to issue a snappy salute. He read the charge: "Airman Fersht, you've been charged with smoking a cigarette in Airplane Hangar such-and-such whilst on active duty Thursday afternoon last. How do you plead?"

I could not believe my ears. "Thursday afternoon." *Gotcha!* I'd found my out—or, rather, it had found me. The charge as specified was in error. *Sergeant Russell, wherever you are, bless you!* "Not guilty, Sir," I replied, striving to project an air of confidence.

Standing to the side, Lieutenant Harris, the charging officer, snorted with disgust. I pretended not to take notice. The CO looked up from the sheaf of papers clutched in his hand and repeated the charge. "Perhaps you didn't hear me right the first time, Airman Fersht," he growled. "How do you plead?"

"Not guilty," I repeated. After all, in for a pence, in for a pound.

"And how is that?" demanded the CO. "Are you saying Lieutenant Harris here has offered false testimony? Do you dare make that assertion?"

"Not at all, Sir," said I. "It just so happens that on the day in question, I was away on pass. Off the base. Nowhere near, Sir. Couldn't have been me."

You could hear a pin drop. The date typed on the charge sheet was off by one. Records proved that I had indeed *not* been on active duty that Thursday. Grudgingly, with a look that said to me "don't ever let something like this happen again, or you're in for you-know-what," the CO smacked the palm of a hand hard against the surface of his desk and barked, "Case dismissed!"

## "Over There"

Unhappy with my quotidian diet of rote repetition of commonplace chores, I repeatedly applied to take RAF-led courses in various supportive trades. Again, the CO stood in the way, preferring preservation of the status quo.

It took no less than eighteen long months for me to finally figure out how to get reassigned to a venue where I could do something—anything, anywhere—to relieve the monotony and enable me to feel like I was truly making a difference. I volunteered for overseas service.

After that, the creaky flywheels of military bureaucracy flew like greased lightning. Others might have been cowed or alarmed by the alacrity with which my transfer orders were processed, but I was no longer the same timid soul who, growing up, couldn't say boo to a goose. Far from it. *Bring it on*, I cheered. *Bring it on*.

## A Passage to War

The year is now 1942. As of March 24, I am twenty-one. The arc of my youth is behind me. A stunted education. Orphaned at fourteen in the throes of the Great Depression. Obliged by circumstance and custom to enter the labor force. Endurance for years of long hours, pathetically substandard working conditions, and meager pay. Caught up with the rest of London, Great Britain, and lands across the entire planet in the sudden eruption of global conflict visited literally upon our doorstep. Enlistment in the Royal Air Force. Boot camp. Then Driffield. Now, off to ultimate destinations unknown. Destinations to be determined by the needs of the service, the luck of the draw, or the whim of a faceless clerk sandwiched somewhere within the bureaucracy where such minute yet epochal decisions are made.

I am twenty-one. The person in the mirror who shaves my face in the morning bears only a skin-deep resemblance to the *bar mitzvah* boy of 1934. That lad is gone. Long gone. In his stead, there stands a man. A serviceman with a passage to war.

As I and others with newly issued travel warrants gather trackside, awaiting arrival of the iron horse that will carry us cross-country, WSW, all the way to the port city of Liverpool, there is much to talk about. Yet little is said. We're preoccupied with the vast imponderables of what may come next.

From Liverpool, we are bused by military transport to a transit exchange depot. There, we are advised to expect new orders, uniforms, and travel vouchers. "From now on," we're admonished, "silence is golden. You'll say nothing to anyone about where you serve, where you're going, nothing. Loose lips sink ships." That much we know already. Our merchant marine vessels and troop carriers are prey to marauding Jerry U-boats in the North Atlantic and the Mediterranean.

So, yes, the warning to keep mum was unquestionably critically important. Yet, it was also technically unnecessary. Though rumors abounded, we hadn't the foggiest where our next post of duty might be.

One clue, a big one to our simple way of thinking, was when we found ourselves being kitted out with tropical weight uniforms. Speculation was rife. Equatorial Africa? The sands of the Middle East? Somewhere in the exotic Far East, of which we knew little or nothing?

Being experienced as I was in the crafts of the garment industry, I could not help but concede mocking admiration for the RAF's feeble attempt at bespoke tailoring. There were three sizes from which to choose: small, medium, large. Three sizes to fit all, regardless of fit. Mine would have been perfect, had my actual crotch hung down below my knees.

The duds included linen shorts, tunic shirts, light underwear, sturdy shoes, and pith helmet. *Cor blimey, a pith helmet!* Only one

I'd ever seen before had been sported by Errol Flynn and cohorts in the cinema six years prior. There he was, starring as Captain Vickers in Warner Bros. *The Charge of the Light Brigade*, fighting valiantly for love and country. What did Flynn have? Olivia de Havilland. What did I have? Clothing that, for lack of belt or braces, would cascade immediately to adorn my feet and ankles.

Imagine a batch of freshly minted soldiers, lads and men who could be their uncles or fathers, parading around the changing room like clowns, adorned with ridiculous-looking pith helmets and either absurdly floppy or torso-strangulating clothing. Pure hilarity. On a still night, such side-bursting laughter as issued forth might have been heard all the way south to Piccadilly.

At length, after copious complaining to the quartermaster, he permitted us to engage in a barter system of sorts. Arrayed in an irregular circle, we did our best to exchange articles piece by piece until a reasonably superior alignment of size and stature had been accomplished. A comedy of errors had been resolved, somewhat, through good-spirited improvisation – a priceless talent when serving in uniform. At a minimum, the exercise took our minds off unspoken misgivings regarding our imminent exposure to the menacing perils of the open sea.

### An Armada to Who Knows Where

Blood pressures, I can assure you, were at an all-time high as orders to assemble at the quayside marshalling area were posted and distributed. We knew not yet where we were going – only that we were, with absolute certainty, about to depart British soil.

The scene is ingrained in my mind's eye: troops arriving en masse via various forms of transport converge to prepare to board one of the many imposing vessels that will carry them forth, taking the war to the enemy. The congregation swells into the thousands as railcars, military vehicles, city buses, and other conveyances pressed into service deposit their human cargoes dockside.

I am in awe. I don't think I'm likely to witness such a spectacle ever again. Stretching as far as the eye can see, a vast armada of massive passenger ships readies to receive us, taking on fuel, materiel, and provisions. Stevedores wrangling heavily laden pallets shout to be heard above the general level of pervasive, unceasing din. All along the waterfront and into the far distance, soldiers, sailors, and airmen, bent over under the weight of overstuffed kit bags, ascend the boarding gangways.

There are no public displays of patriotic pride in sending these lads off to war. No banners, or bunting, or bands. Word of the undertaking has been held tightly. Troops have been under orders to keep mum – even from Mum and Dad. *Loose Lips Sink Ships.*

My orders are to board the *Stirling Castle*, a seven-year-old converted ocean liner, cargo and Royal Mail carrier built and first launched in Belfast, Northern Ireland. Powered by twin Burmeister & Wain 10-cylinder diesel engines, she is capable of hitting a brisk twenty knots.

I take my place in line, advance to the threshold of the gangplank, lift one foot, and then the other, off solid land. There's no way to know, not the faintest of inklings, that my feet might not and will not become planted on the *terra firma* of our island nation again until the war is won, many years hence.

## A High Seas Village

In her infancy, the *Stirling Castle* regularly carried upwards of twelve hundred passengers and crew, along with freight and Royal Mail deliveries, from Southampton to Cape Town, South Africa, and back, setting speed records in the process.

Amenities abounded, as did the incorporation of advanced technologies in lighting, fire detection and suppression systems, cargo refrigeration, double-hull construction, engine design, and reserve power generation.[12]

---

[12] R.M.M.V. "Stirling Castle", *Shipping Wonders of the World* (Part 41, Nov. 17, 1936). Illustration by Henry Hudson Rodmell. Source: http://www.shippingwondersoftheworld.com/part41.html.

Prior to her having been requisitioned for wartime service, the ship's first class customers had their pick of how and where to while away the hours. Their section featured a formal dining area; card, drawing, and smoking rooms; a veranda; a gymnasium; a cinema; and even a swimming pool.

To accommodate her newest voyagers, however, many of the *Stirling Castle*'s interior flourishes, in first class and throughout the ship, had been removed. Nonetheless, though we of the lower ranks were restricted in our movements, with certain zones having been made accessible only to NCOs and officers, evidence of the ship's grace and beauty were everywhere to be seen.

Such aesthetics and creature comforts as there were, however, were either of no consequence to our daily routines or largely unavailable to the ordinary enlisted man – of which there were thousands jammed in a space designed for a fraction of that number. The ship that was – a pleasure craft transporting *bons vivants* to new adventures and home again – has gone to war. We troops have replaced her tourists. She has become a compact, water-borne, high-density village of missionaries, taking the battle to the enemy. She has been staffed and stocked to be totally self-sufficient, with one exception, one critical dependency: the blanket of protection afforded by our convoy's escort vessels, ever vigilant in hostile waters. They numbered in the high twenties to low thirties. *Thank you, good neighbors, and Godspeed.*

## A Day in the Life

With a faint glow signaling the approach of sunrise on the starboard horizon, we begin the day with a lifeboat drill. Troops on each deck have been divided into units with designated assembly points. It doesn't help my psyche to know inside that I never learned how to swim. I admit that small detail to no one; hardly even to myself.

Naval gunners fore and aft test their deck-mounted machine guns, blazing them into the sky, shattering the air and assaulting our eardrums with soundwaves of heavy rolling thunder.

Next, we'll be off for a round of physical training exercises – and all of this before breakfast.

Instructional lectures run the gamut from the mundane to matters of survival. We're sensitized to cultural differences and specific do's and don'ts for the country we're about to enter. Certain nuances of the spoken word and of body language can have significant consequences. We listen and take mental note. There are lessons in the proper use and care of weaponry when subject to varying environmental conditions. Salt air, dampness, sand, and fine particles of dust are hazards that, if not scrupulously guarded against, may spell the difference between reliable operational performance and death. We listen and take heed. Admonitions regarding personal hygiene are serious affairs as well. The feet are particularly susceptible to debilitating fungal disease and infection if not kept clean and dry. We endure the usual obligatory warnings regarding sexually transmitted diseases. Some snicker when they hear that there are prostitutes ready to receive them in port. "If you must," one of our priestly taskmasters advises with a disapproving purse of the lips, "don't be stupid. Wear a jacket." *What kind of jacket, guv? A Harris Tweed?*

Our activities and responsibilities are minutely orchestrated and informed via the posting of *DROs – Daily Routine Orders*. Every twenty-four hours, like clockwork, we report to our squadron leader's office to determine who-does-what and when.

On a given morning, I am assigned to serve as a dining room orderly. The duty affords me the opportunity to witness and participate in a process mind-boggling in scope and complexity: that of the logistics and mechanics of feeding of thousands of stomachs three times a day.

My delivery of prepared meals to tables where ravenous airmen attack and denude the platters as soon as they hit the deck is but the final act. The process begins within the bowels of the ship with orders issued by the purveyor's office.

The arena of activity is vast and, being devoid of sunlight, cavernous. Jeeps carrying foodstuffs loaded within gated storage facilities shuttle to elevators which raise them to upper deck platforms where galley staff unload and transport the cargos to their respective food preparation stations. There are all manner of cooks standing post, each with a particular specialty. They do their best to make appetizing meals on a production line basis. Not an easy task. As one expects to see in a four-star hotel, they wear the uniform of a chef: white linen coveralls and a tall white crown. The impression of the inner workings of a mega-hotel is further enhanced by associated operations on a grand scale: dishwashing, laundry, refuse collection and disposal.

The experience earns my great respect still today for those who serve in a support capacity, laboring repetitiously and tirelessly, virtually round the clock, day after day, to sustain body and morale. My hat's off to them.

## Can't Complain

After having participated in *Operation Feed Me*, I can't complain about the shortcomings of our temporary accommodations. (Well, actually, I can complain, but who would listen?) Unlike the aforementioned four-star hotel, where one might hope to turn in for the night on a queen-size Queen Anne four-poster, there are no beds here. No firm horizontal surfaces on which to unfurl a bedroll. Nothing of the sort. We sleep in hammocks, padded saggy sacks of knotted netting which pitch and roll with the undulating movements of the ship.

Mounting these contraptions is no picnic. They're hung on hooks that suspend them well off the deck, to the extent that one must execute a precision leap in order to gain purchase and catapult into the center. A near miss can prove to be quite painful. Set about eighteen inches apart, they afford but nine inches of sway before colliding with an adjacent hammock if it happens to be swinging in the opposite direction.

As space is at a premium and serves multiple uses during the course of the day, hammocks must be unmounted and stowed each morning, along with one's kit, to free up the 'barracks' for whatever comes next.

Food is rationed. Smokes are rationed. Space is rationed. One commodity that is *not* rationed is shower water. There's plenty of it. Plenty of *saltwater*, that is. The sensation is that of cleansing oneself with an oil slick. Saltwater refuses to enable soap to develop a lather, and even after one has toweled off, the skin feels sticky to the touch.

I remind myself: if the cooks don't complain, how can I?

## From Pollywog to Shellback

Equatorial line-crossing rituals in the British Royal Navy have roots that go back at least to the era of James Cook, who captained the *Endeavour* to the Pacific in 1768. They serve as jovial morale-boosting ceremonies in which those who have not previously crossed the equator are initiated into the ranks of those who have. King Neptune, bedecked in royal robes, passes judgment on each of a select group of first-timers, greenhorn *Pollywogs*. One by one, lined up along the length of the swimming pool diving board, they plunge into the deep end, clothes on, and emerge as veterans of the crossing, members of the *Ancient Order of the Shellbacks*.

Back in Captain Cook's day, repeated immersion and dunking was directly into the briny depths. Here, no such hazardous hazing is in the offing. Though the proceedings are conducted with pomp and feigned seriousness of purpose, frivolity is the order of the day. I, along with the rest of the ship's complement of enlisted men, look on as the officers have their fun. Nevertheless, this first-crossing airman-sailor feels a swell of pride at the accomplishment. I am no longer a seagoing whelp. I am a Shellback.

## Repose and Reflection

Months before, whilst grinding out the regimens of boot camp, there'd been no opportunity to avail myself of the quiet pleasures of the quaint fishing village of Arbroath. No interludes of repose and reflection. Arbroath might as well have been on the moon.

Within the confines of the floating village of the *Stirling Castle*, however, I did manage to find such moments, either before reveille or at dusk. Standing alone in a quiet spot, snug up against her rails, I would peer into the darkness, diluted in the wee hours as the earth turns toward the sun, but near pitch black on still moonless nights punctuated only by starlight and the faint running lights of a fleet vessel. There were fewer guardian escort vessels, as our convoy had made it past the prime hunting grounds of Nazi *Kriegsmarine U-Boot* wolf packs and into the broad Atlantic, zig-zagging unpredictably all along the way.

As the *Castle* churned ahead into the wind, sea breezes washed over me, refreshing and replenishing. Waves splashed and slapped against the sides of the ship rhythmically. Our twin turbines, powering us forward, vibrated and resonated with strength and conviction. They were the reassuring context of the otherwise silent darkness.

As the predawn hour waned, I would await the arrival of the great orange orb, peeping the edge of the world on the far eastern horizon. Occasionally, flashes of light burst in the distance as convoy ships signaled messages to one another.

I allowed my thoughts to drift and stray. I thought of home and family. Parents and youth. Celia and Kitty and all the others. I was twenty-one. What would the immediate future hold for me?

On my last leave before shipping out, I made no mention of my overseas posting, though I did say to Celia that she would likely not be hearing from me for a while. She knew. I could tell. But she wouldn't invite an indiscretion on my part by asking outright.

Dawn broke in the vast, landless expanses of the Atlantic. Without reference points or manmade haze to filter its rays, the sun appeared to be enormous, as if it could swallow us whole.

My thoughts returned to dear sister Celia. How difficult it must have been for her and the family to accept that fact that I, their 'baby' brother, was heading into harm's way. Suddenly, on impulse, I looked down into the forbidding darkness of the ocean deep. The specter of U-Boats knocked at the door, demanding to be admitted. To dwell on such dread possibilities would be to invite disaster. With a snort and a wave of the hand, I dismissed the uninvited, malevolent intrusion. One has to do that. It's part of the survival instinct.

## Land, Ho!

After many long days at sea, buffeted by rolling waves and relentless routine, we pined for a shout of *land, ho!* And then, hallelujah, it came. I can hear and see it now.

We espy what we take to be a coastline, if our eyes are not deceiving us. It is not a mirage. It grows more and more real by the minute. We've been treated somewhat as mushrooms, nurtured yet kept in dark until there's a need to know. Now there is. We're sprinting along the northwest coast of Africa, on our way toward the Gold Coast, a longtime British colony on the Gulf of Guinea. We're going to be putting in beforehand, briefly, at the port of Freetown, Liberia. For most of us, Africa has been the stuff of lore, legend, and history books. An abstraction. Dark-skinned inhabitants. Exotic animals. Thick jungles. Tarzan. Stanley and Livingston.

The harbor is too shallow to accommodate our ship. We drop anchor in the bay. Along with several airmen, I am dispatched to lend a hand below. Massive steel doors at the side of the ship have been opened to receive incoming supplies. In the distance, we spot a cargo-carrying motorboat heading our way.

After an exchange of recognition signals, the vessel pulls alongside. Permission is granted for members of the crew to climb aboard. "With our compliments to your captain," one of them says, indicating a stack of crated fresh fruits to be hoisted on board. Later, I learn that such acts of hospitality are an engrained element of naval tradition.

I help myself to one of them and ask its name. "It's a mango,"

I'm told. The specimen looks, feels, and smells different from anything I've ever encountered before. At first, I try cutting through it. No luck. I keep hacking at it, unaware there is a large, near impenetrable nut at the center. By the time I'm finished, I've reduced the object to an ugly pulp. But, oh, that flavor. Ripe, succulent, sweet, and tangy, it dances on the tongue. My mouth and chin are dripping with the thick nectar of my first tropical fruit.

On my return to top deck, everyone seems to be crowded around the rails as grinning natives paddle alongside in their canoes, clamoring for *bucksheesh* – for small gratuities in the form of British coin currency. They put on quite a performance as they dive to retrieve pocket change tossed into the brink before it disappears into the murk.

Some of them make a fuss: pennies are not worth the trouble. They insist we step up with pieces of silver. Some of our men put their creative, larcenous talents to good use by wrapping tuppence with glittery tinfoil paper lining nipped from a packet of *Players* cigarettes. Another round of diving-for-treasure ensues, but the would-be dupes aren't gulled so easily. They quickly discover the ruse and let their ire be known: "You fuck me up, you bastards."

It appears that our brothers-in-arms, British servicemen bivouacked in Africa's friendly ports, have been doing their level best to enrich international relations by introducing the aborigines to the refined high art of the English language.

## A Friendly Port

We are well underway again, making good progress, though to which ultimate station we can only speculate – and will not be made privy to until that destination is nigh upon us.

The days pass unremarkably – a good thing. Then, on the eve of our prospective arrival, we are informed at last: Cape Town. Capital of South Africa. Friendly territory.[13]

---

[13] Immediately after Hitler's invasion of Poland, South Africa's legislative body deposed its neutrality-leaning prime minister and rallied around Jan Smuts, a

With but one evening's travel time separating the *Stirling Castle* from anchorage at Cape Town, I bed down for the night, slung in the hammock, daydreaming of what it will be like to put my feet on solid, hospitable ground again.

As I'm habituated to rising early, when little else is going on, I'm also attuned to the mechanical and organic sounds and vibrations of the ship. Something is decidedly different. The engines – much, much quieter – have settled into a rhythmic hum. I hasten to make my way up top and a portside perch. Except for the ever-so-gentle rippling of harbor waters, nothing else seems to be in motion. Sometime during wee hours, we'd dropped anchor in Table Bay.

Once again, I've beaten the sun. Alone and quiet as a church mouse, I hold fast to the rail, dwarfed by an immense, enveloping jet black sky above. Suddenly, smack dab on the horizon, an arc of radiant light erupts, a fiery palette of rainbow colors which I delight in believing is a welcome sign displayed just for me.

With the break of dawn, I take it all in. The skyline is dominated by the rugged silhouette of the city's iconic *Tafelberg – Table Mountain*, literally, in the tongue of the region's *Afrikaans* colonizers. All at once, its flat-topped expanse is set ablaze, backlit by a flaming crimson sphere which climbs *Tafelberg*'s peaks.

Then, as if responding to a wake-up call, the town appears to come to life for the commerce of the day as electric lights looking for all the world like starbursts start popping up all over. The sun's ascendancy, coupled with the brilliance of a thriving seaport twinkling hello, is the most spectacular, beautiful sight I have ever seen, destined never to fade from memory.

---

highly decorated soldier and statesman, to lead a new coalition government. On September 4, 1939, the country's reconstituted parliament declared war on the Axis powers, thus committing to the Allied cause.

## Cape Town

The ship's engines come to life again. From the bridge, the captain directs the *Stirling Castle* to her dockside berth with the aid of a pilot vessel assigned by the harbor master. Others join me at the rail. The rush of anticipation is palpable. Dry land. Allies. Hot meals. Real beds. Women.

Cape Town's strategic importance in controlling the sea lanes rounding the Cape of Good Hope makes our mission vital, if not essential, to the Allies' success within our theater of operations. We are one of the first RAF contingents to make land here, and we will be most welcome, as local manpower eligible for enlistment is at a premium.

For those not tasked via the *DROs* with performing specific duties on any given day, twenty-four hours' shore leave is granted. On Day One, I am free to go explore the town. As I descend the gangplank, eager to step ashore for the first time on foreign (yet friendly) soil, my heart beats with the excitement of a child about to experience his first carnival.

Though we've been briefed, so to speak, by lectures regarding the customs, cultures, and mores of our host country, we are relatively unschooled in how to deal with challenging situations which may arise from the realities on the ground. The country is a land of haves and have-nots. A land where *apartheid* separates the races. A politically charged milieu in which Nazi sympathizers have striven to thwart the nation's pact with the Allies through skullduggery and sabotage. South Africa is not London, England.

At dockside, I turn to look up at the imposing figure of the *Stirling Castle*. When on board, I came to feel that I had taken her measure, that her compact universe was one that I had mastered in wending my way from assignment to assignment throughout the length, breadth, and depth of her being. Now, staring up, up, up to her top deck and craning my neck to admire the proud forward thrust of her prow, I am humbled. She is a magnificent machine that carried us safely from hemisphere to hemisphere, from latitudes 50° North to 33° South. *Thank you, noble lady.*

## Boys at Heart

Early on during the course of our journey, I met a fellow airman named Sonny Ribbler, a Scotsman who also happened to be Jewish. We became best friends. You haven't lived until your ears try to adjust to and interpret the words and sounds of a voice speaking with a Scottish Yiddish accent. At first, it was not unlike conversing with an extra-terrestrial. For anyone today who happens to be a *Star Trek* fan, think *Klingon*.

On our first night out, Sonny and I had several libations at one of the many saloons dotting the Cape Town waterfront. We were in a jovial mood, feeling no pain, as they say. Time got away from us. We hurriedly returned to the ship, hustled on board, located our below-deck quarters, grabbed hammocks from the stow, hooked up, clambered into the sack, and fell fast asleep.

The next morning, we were surprised to find that in our absence, the crew had seen fit to rearrange everything. Nothing looked familiar. Neither the size nor arrangement of the room. Not the corridors of the ship. Not even the people.

*What's going on?* we wondered in our hungover state. *Where the bloody hell are we?* "Not the *Stirling Castle*, you silly sods," answered a petty officer, shaking his head in disbelief.

In our defense, all ships of substance look alike at night, cloaked in darkness, to well-lubricated brains that have lost their ability to discriminate amongst the behemoths.


## Transit Camp

We soon learned to make the most of our frequent daily passes, making sure as well that we managed to return to no other ship than the *Castle* at the end of a day's explorations and revelry!

Then came new orders. We were being moved to a new location, *Retreat*, twenty-some kilometers due south of Cape Town, where a tented transit camp pitched in a parched, desert-like expanse awaited our contingent. The name *Retreat*, we learned much later, had been earned in 1795 as a consequence of the *Battle of Muizenberg*, a skirmish between the British and *Afrikaner* descendants of the original Dutch settlers of southern Africa, both vying for control of the seagoing trade routes between East and West. Who wanted to be bivouacked at a place bearing such a moniker, no matter who'd been the bested party? Not us.

Nor did we appreciate the admonition to prepare our cots for a night's sleep only when actually ready to turn in – and to do so with tight hospital corners. Scorpion denizens of the patch, we were told, are quite adept at finding their way under blankets to cuddle up next to warm bodies and, on occasion, make their presence known with a lash of the tail.

The one amazing bright spot in camp living was the incredible abundance of food—of meat in particular – cooked by tall, massively husky natives standing over piping hot stone ranges. At dinnertime, barbecued steaks weighing at least two pounds apiece, seared and sizzling, released aromas that drove us nuts.

Salivating, we eagerly queued to receive our 'ration.' As each of our turns came, the towering chef would spear a perfectly charred slab and swing it in one mighty arc plop onto the mess tin. If you weren't holding your tray in a death grip by both hands, the whole shebang would shoot to the ground, and you've have to make do with beef à la sand.

Next to each grill stood a large, brand new galvanized refuse bin filled to the brim with fully cooked potatoes, each of them Amazonian in size.

The sheer abundance of outsized portions struck me as unreal and, to an extent, unfair. I couldn't help but think about the privations being endured back home. There, had such a thing as a two-pound serving of decent meat been made available in the marketplace or at the local butcher's, it would likely have been stretched to feed sixteen people on a month's ration coupons.

Camp breakfast was equally lavish in terms of volume. When it came to bacon-and-eggs, my cherished early morning sentry duty treat from days at Driffield, I could help myself to as much as I could possibly eat. And that I did that first time through, loading my mess tin with a heaping mound of rashers and scramble. Oh, happy appetite! Worthy of whistling *The White Cliffs of Dover* on my way to the dining tent.

Until the impossible happened. I'd been blissfully unaware that vigilant predators – avian raptors – loomed way overhead, circling the periphery of our open-air cafeteria, as ready to pounce as a tiger concealed in savanna tall grass. Indigenous, hawk-like, black-shouldered kites had become thoroughly adept in the art and science of opportunistic aerial thievery. As I made my merry way across the compound, a feathered beast with a three-foot wingspan, casting a looming shadow over my own, swooped in, snagged a fat tangle of bacon strips with adhered chunks of yolky egg within its needle-sharp, grasping talons, and zoomed skyward, all in one startlingly swift, fluid motion. I was speechless. *Cannibal!* I should have cried.

"Here there," piped up one of the camp veterans, having witnessed my loss and my loss for words. "The trick, mate, is to wave a hand and flutter the fingertips over top your platter, back-and-forth, constantly. Like this," he demonstrated. "The movements alarm and confuse the nasty things. Keeps them from stealing your grub. So then they go after somebody who isn't that clever – like you just now."


## The Goldbergs

When we first arrived in South Africa and began sampling Cape Town's offerings, we always nightcapped the day at one of the many service personnel canteens where blokes such as I congregated for a friendly face, a cup of cheer, a song of home, and chance to—what do you think? To meet girls. Local lasses aside, however, it was at one such establishment that Sonny Ribbler and I soon made the acquaintance of one of their volunteers: a remarkable lady, Mrs. Ruth Tannenbaum Goldberg.

I should say, however, that it was *she* who made *our* acquaintance, either by chance or by some uncanny intuition on her part that we were of the Jewish faith, for it was she who approached and introduced herself to us. We hit it off immediately and wound up chatting on and on, sharing stories of our backgrounds and how we came to be service to crown and country. At evening's end, she invited us to come meet her family at home on our next outing.

And that we did. To our surprise and delight, it was as if we'd found ourselves in the midst of long-lost, warm-hearted relatives. Before we had a chance to sit down, Mrs. Goldberg asked us to come back into the kitchen and meet her housekeeper. "Minnie," she said, "these airmen are from Britain, and we must treat them like family whenever they visit. One thing for sure, they'll never leave here hungry." With that, she turned, opened the cupboards, and declared, "Please, boys, do help yourselves."

Her husband, Isaiah Goldberg, was most welcoming and generous, too. He and Ruth owned and operated a small business where they printed Jewish New Year cards. Their modest home was called *Harmony,* after the neighborhood in which they resided. *How very appropriate*, I remember thinking at the time.

Soon we were to meet the entire family as our visits become more frequent. On one such occasion, we were introduced to a nephew about my age, and we hit it off right away – so much so that our hijinks eventually found us wrestling on the lawn. We saw that Mrs. Goldberg seemed to be enjoying the moment as much as we were. She stood laughing on the front porch, snapping pictures of our carefree horseplay with a Kodak *Brownie* camera.

Four years later—four incredibly long years that transpired with the slow-motion surrealism of an often nightmarish dream—after I'd been discharged from duties and returned home, I came across one of those snapshots in a batch that sister Celia had lovingly preserved in prayerful anticipation of my eventual return. I couldn't believe my eyes.

"How ever did you get this?" I asked. "It came in the post," she replied.

I was bowled over, having had no recollection of providing Mrs. Goldberg with Celia's address. The good lady must have gone to great lengths to determine that all on her own, an act of tenderhearted consideration which speaks volumes about her abiding maternal nature and deep appreciation for the ties that bind.

As I studied the photograph, it took on dimension and took me back to those fleeting days in Cape Town. My wrestling partner, Joel Goldberg, had been engaged to be married. He had insisted that Sonny and I attend the wedding. We were able to do so only after having bartered an exchange of on-duty assignments with others in our squadron. Unfortunately, though, by the time we arrived at the private home where the reception was being held, both the wedding ceremony and the dinner that followed had ended. We'd knocked on the door just in time to be admitted for the onset of a time-honored British tradition: a long line of longwinded speeches.

Nonetheless, the hosts hastily organized platters of food for us as we respectfully took seats for the obligatory rounds of testimonials and toasts. In the meantime, Joel, looking every inch the beaming newlywed groom, stood and proceeded to quiet the assembly.

"Please," he said, "I'd like to say a few words. First, let me introduce Sidney Fersht and Sonny Ribbler, sitting over here – raise your hands fellows." We complied, somewhat shyly. "These two young men, at great personal risk, have braved the Atlantic to come here in defense of our country and the free world."

A round of applause and cries of 'hear-hear' ensued. "Furthermore," Joel continued, "I happen to know that our special day also happens to be Sonny Ribbler's birthday – so let's raise our glasses and extend our best wishes for a long and happy life!" We misted up as they sang *Happy Birthday*.

In reminiscing now, I am able to count the ten weeks we spent in South Africa as amongst the happiest passages of my life, thanks to the Goldbergs and their marvelous extended family.

## A Passage to India

Transit camp *Retreat* had been precisely that: a waystation in our multi-phase journey to service in India. Again, we would not come to know that with absolute certainty until on the verge of arriving there. The ship engaged to transport us on the next leg was in many ways the antithesis of the grand *Stirling Castle*. It was a leaky old bucket that, to our consternation, spewed a steady, heavy stream of seawater constantly from drainage conduits on the starboard side of the ship as overworked bilge pumps labored to rid the hull of nonstop seepage. The thrum of those pumps could be heard and felt all the way from Cape Town, round the Cape of Good Hope, past Port Elizabeth, and on to Durban, our next port of call.

After Cape Town, Durban couldn't help but be a complete letdown. My recollection of our ten-day layover there is a blur, with the exception of my having stood guard at a *Woolworth* emporium that had, for whatever reason, been identified as a high priority asset to be protected round the clock against depredations by thieves and black marketeers.

When it came time to board another troop carrier for a crossing of the Indian Ocean, we got wise. With a high degree of probability, how could our destination not be Bombay? We braced for another lengthy waterborne trek, thirty-eight hundred nautical miles northeast from Durban.

## An Ancient Civilization

There's a famously familiar epigram that goes: 'East is East, and West is West, and never the twain shall meet.' It was penned by Rudyard Kipling in his poem *The Ballad of East and West*. The first four lines read:

Oh, East is East, and West is West, and never the twain shall meet,

Till Earth and Sky stand presently at God's great Judgment Seat;

But there is neither East nor West, Border, nor Breed, nor Birth,

When two strong men stand face to face, though they come from the ends of the earth!

Oh, how he got that one right! In my twenty-first year, I suddenly found myself amongst peoples whose cultures, customs, and modes of everyday living were unlike anything I'd been led to believe or could possibly have imagined. I felt as if I *had* traveled from one end of the earth to another, where ancient civilizations continued to thrive despite the march of time.

For the reader to understand and appreciate better the ensuing narrative of my adventures and observations, it is important to provide some basic historical background and context.

At the outbreak of World War II, India, a 'protectorate nation' subject to Crown Rule since the middle of the 19th century, had a population of approximately 380 million – fully one-sixth of the world's 2.3 billion – dwarfing the United Kingdom's 48 million, and greater than that of the Empire of Japan, the Republic of China, the Soviet Union, and the United States, individually.

The country was steeped – some might say mired – in caste system traditions and strictures that had evolved and become engrained in the fabric of society throughout hundreds and thousands of years. Differences in religion, region, profession, and family ranking at birth determined or severely constrained opportunity, mobility, legal status, and other salient aspects of life.

Linguistically as well, India was a non-melting pot with a plethora of distinct languages and scripts, plus dialects running to the high hundreds. Though the country bore one name, India, it was anything but unified in terms of national identity, direction, and vision for the future.

Add to those structural impediments the overlay of a world at war, plus Mahatma Gandhi's *Quit India Movement* calling for British withdrawal – launched in Bombay on August 8, 1942 – and a perfect storm emerged of volatile, countervailing forces impinging simultaneously as we RAF airmen were delivered to her shores.

## Bombay

The port at Bombay had all the trappings of an immense, sprawling overpopulated city. From our top deck vantage point high above the shoreline, the scenes were those of hordes of people going about their business, unfazed by jumbled pathways packed thick with shoppers and vendors, the high decibel clatter and rumble of commotion, and the sheer madness of it all. Certainly, in the absence of any evidence of interest or curiosity on their part, they seemed oblivious to the arrival of yet another gigantic troopship brimming with thousands of soldiers pressing the rails to catch their first glimpse of the storied realm of the British Raj.

I was among those angling for a better view of the cityscape. The docklands were capable of servicing some of the largest ships to enter their waters, ours included. Captain and crew negotiated the densely packed harbor and maneuvered our vessel into its assigned berth with ease and efficiency that belied the extent of the challenge.. Their knowledge of tides, currents, wind speed and direction, channel depths, and dockside conditions – all of those had to be considered in determining how and when to adjust course headings and ship speeds to achieve the one and only best result. Anything less would be to court disaster. My admiration was such that I never took their expertise – and courage – for granted.

With shore passes in hand, Sonny Ribbler and I, along with a few other airmen, made our way down the gangway, only to find ourselves at a loss as to what to do next. We didn't have the slightest idea where to go. One of the ship's crew, a seasoned sailor who knew the port like the back of his hand, noticed our bewilderment and offered to be our guide. We thanked him and followed his lead, snaking and zigzagging our way hither and yon in such a way that retracing our steps would have taken a miracle.

It shouldn't have come as a surprise to us, then, to discover that our navy man had, at length, ushered his wide-eyed retinue of air force landlubbers into the port's seamy red light district and its not-so-forbidden gardens of earthly pursuits.

If, dear reader, you've never had the dubious pleasure of visiting a brothel, let me assure you that it's not anything akin to the stylized, sanitized renderings typically depicted in theatrical films and television dramas. I was no prude, mind you, but I was not prepared for what I saw: a shamelessly paraded supermarket of women, many of them of school age, either needing to offer their bodies for rent in order to survive or being forced to do so.

Their garments were shabby. Even after their overseer, a corpulent matron acting the part of 'madam' ostentatiously, had them change into brightly colored, relatively clean saris and parade seductively before us, they appeared forlorn. The sight filled me with both revulsion and compassion. Maybe having been the youngest of nine siblings, five of whom were female and all of whom deserved to be treated with dignity, I was particularly susceptible to feelings of empathy for the plight of those not born into better circumstances.

Even had I craved the warmth of womanly companionship I could not possibly have availed myself of a tumble in a whorehouse and thereafter have hoped to maintain a shred of self-respect. Any one of those women could have been a Celia, a Freda, a Hettie, a Sue, or a Kitty—in some other family, to some younger brother.

I excused myself, left the premises, and waited outside until my companions had finished their business. Afterwards, they did not question or tease me about my sensibilities.

Once again, we found ourselves caught up in the boiling commerce of the waterfront. It was there and then that I became initiated into an entirely different rite of passage: that of engaging and enjoying my first rickshaw ride. In all of India's larger metropolitan areas, rickshaws were the most efficient, preferred modes of personal transportation. Think of a dumbed-down Irish trap being pulled by a human being instead of a horse, and there you have your basic rickshaw.

I was fascinated to watch and learn how their owner-operator entrepreneurs mastered the science of two-wheeled, two-footed locomotion. They sprint, run, or gallop, depending on traffic conditions, while pulling the carriage by elongated handles tucked under the arms. Their strides are long and loping, generating energy-conserving rhythm and momentum. When legitimate pathways become too congested or inhospitable to movement by rickshaw, they think nothing of intruding on sidewalks or any other patch of level ground, obviously being immune to sharp objections and occasional virulent curses voiced by inconvenienced and endangered pedestrians.

## Stark Contrasts

After my first few days on Indian soil, I began to realize that my formative impressions of the country – the reasons why it seemed so utterly foreign to the European (to this particular British European, I should say) – weren't the obvious ones. Not the crowded conditions. Not the unfamiliar modes of dress. Not the widespread poverty. One finds them in metropolises all over the world. Yes, Indian men and women were attired quite differently, clothed mostly in linens wrapped around the torso or draped over the shoulders. Yes, the hustle-and-bustle was intense and often, to my unaccustomed Western eyes, chaotic. And yes, beggary was endemic.

But when I asked myself why India, a cultured civilization through millennia and a British protectorate for the better part of a century, struck me as so dramatically at variance with fundamental *a priori* expectations, it was none of those facets *per se*. It was the sheer magnitude of the starkness of contrasts. The jarring juxtaposition of the ancient and the modern. The arguably unbridgeable gulf between the haves and have-nots. The bottomless pits of abject poverty coexisting cheek-by-jowl with havens of the privileged elite. Were these polar opposites the inevitable products of a caste society?

One moment I'd be strolling along a street in a thriving, upscale commercial district featuring retail shops, bank buildings, and cinemas – and the next, I'd turn the corner and encounter slum conditions absolutely unimaginable back home. The filthiest dregs of human society. Hollow-eyed women in cages, being hawked to pleasure men for pennies. Deformed children, their arms and legs twisted and maimed, either at childbirth or, worse, through malnutrition and maltreatment, being used as pity props by exploitative handlers – pimps of the worst kind – who stood in the background, waiting like vultures to swoop in and snatch whatever meager pittances might be cast into a cup at the feet of their victimized bait. Boys, inducted by their elders into the flesh market, trained to run alongside British troop vehicles and soldiers on foot, shouting, "*Sahib*! Plenty of *jig-jig*. Have big sister."

## Early Impressions

Whilst in Bombay we were situated in yet another transit camp, awaiting posting to our parent unit. Our duties consisted mainly of sentry details – both there and at assigned external locations – and of daily fatigues, exhausting exercises intended to maintain body tone and build stamina.

One day the *DROs* called for me to guard RAF property awaiting transit at the city's principal railway station, the *Victoria Terminus* – a site notoriously susceptible to pilferage.

Porters, colloquially termed *coolies*, were impossible to ignore or avoid. They swarmed arriving trains, forming what amounted to a human barrier. They were capable of carrying several pieces of luggage at once, objects weighing in the aggregate multiples of their body mass, sometimes with both arms fully laden and another load balanced on the head. At night, disembarking passengers had to contend with hundreds of them as they blanketed the platforms, stretched out to catch some shuteye on makeshift bedding.

It was at the terminal, whilst on guard duty, that I befriended a young Indian about my age who was employed as the fifth assistant to the stationmaster. Though most positions entailed hiring unskilled labor, Manish (pronounced muh-*neesh*) was sufficiently apt to be attending a local college, seeking to secure a brighter future for himself. He told me the only work he could find was with the railway – a job he described as 'slamming doors' on the carriage compartments as the trains were about to depart.

In contrast to that example of underemployment stood the example of the stationmaster himself. Without a doubt, he would have not qualified for such an important managerial post in Great Britain. And yet, either through connections or bribery, he'd secured the plum assignment here. That constituted my first experience with the manifest inequities of British colonialism.

The injustices of wartime are certainly not limited to those committed intentionally. Unintended consequences – instances of 'collateral damage' as the often self-exculpatory expression goes – can be devastating. On one occasion, Sonny Ribbler and I fell into conversation with a woman at a serviceman's canteen, a volunteer who'd been recently widowed. She had escaped Germany in the late 1930s, thanks to having met and married an expatriate Bavarian who was then in the employ of an oil company based in India. We ventured to inquire regarding the circumstances of his untimely death. "He succumbed to a severe case of asthma," she related. "We did have an air conditioner in our apartment, and that seemed to help keep him going." *Did the air conditioner fail?* "No. Sad to say, the British Army confiscated it. They said the unit was desperately needed for the hospital." Sonny and I looked at one another dolefully. "I just hope," she sighed, "it didn't wind up in some officer's quarters or the like. That would be a shame." Indeed it would.

Bombay, destined to be renamed Mumbai in 1995, was a metropolitan bazaar, a vast aggregation of disparate neighborhoods in which anything and everything was made available for a price. My needs were simple: clothing that wouldn't fall down and a decent meal now and again.

One morning, bright and early, I shopped the clothing stalls until I found just the right linen tunic for dress wear, as our standard issue was so ill fitting and clownish that there was no way I was going to be seen flopping around in it. For my one-size-fits-all regulation trousers, with a waist that could accommodate one-

and-a-half of me, I purchased a simple leather belt to replace the coarse length of clothesline rope that I'd pressed into service.

Perhaps it was a bit cheeky of me, a working class lad hailing from a country not celebrated for its stellar cuisine, but I couldn't abide the food dished up in camp. I stuck to the reliable basics: bread and butter, potatoes, and fruit. That diet soon became intolerably monotonous. I asked one of the camp regulars whether he could recommend a good local restaurant for me to try. I was fully prepared to go native. "Yes," he replied, "There's a great little Chinese place that makes the best hot banana and apple fritters ever." Chinese food in India. I had to laugh, but why not give it a go? And was he ever so right! To this day, the recollection of those savory treats makes my mouth water.

I witnessed how differently women were treated in India, and not just those who, as property of their masters, were enslaved in prostitution. One afternoon, as I treated myself to a rare, aimless walkabout, a young couple sitting on the steps of a municipal building caught my attention. They appeared to be newlyweds, judging by their crisp linen outfits and festive appurtenances. His dhoti was draped and wrapped traditional Hindu style, with a length of fabric turned over the shoulder, wound about the torso, and tucked between the legs. Beside him, chatting away, was an older man whom I took to be his father. The bride, bedecked in a bright, colorful sari and adorned with trinkets, sat silently and dutifully behind them, as befitted her position in the family pecking order. One arm was looped through the carry handle of a large straw basket brimming with cooking utensils.

Along came a tattered, horse-drawn hansom cab. With not too much imagination, one could surmise it had seen better times plying the streets of Whitechapel fifty years prior, back in the days when Jack the Ripper had terrorized that part of the East End. In the flatbed rear of the carriage a loose bale of straw served as both fodder for the dray horse and bedding to seat any 'overflow' passengers. Father and son stepped up to settle into the comfort of an upholstered leather bench as the bride, trailing behind them, hoisted herself and all of the young couple's worldly possession into the straw. With the snap of a whip, their journey was underway: a hayride honeymoon, Indian style.

## An Indian Pesach

The festival of *Passover* is celebrated around the world wherever observant Jews may live or travel. India in wartime was no exception. The evening of Monday, April 19, 1943, was *Erev Pesach*, the first night of two that are observed in orthodoxy. Posted on our squadron's *DROs* notice board that morning was an invitation for those of the Jewish faith (and anyone else so desiring) to attend a *Seder* service being conducted by a resident family.

Sonny Ribbler and I decided to accept. Our hosts, a fellow and his young adult daughter, were Middle Eastern *Sephardim* – orthodox Jews of Iberian descent who, in keeping with their branch of Judaism, preserved and practiced rituals rooted in customs going back millennia to the ascendancy of Babylonia. Elements of the service such as the composition of the Seder plate and the practice of eating *maror*, sprigs of bitter herbs dipped in saltwater, to acknowledge the anguish of enslavement and the tears shed by afflicted Hebrews – they, of course, were thoroughly familiar to us. Our hosts' recital of the *Haggadah*, however, was literally incomprehensible, spoken in what we assumed to be classic Hebrew nuanced by Spanish or Portuguese inflection.

We were the only two airmen who'd been 'assigned' to attend their Seder. Our unease arose not only from being totally at sea in the conduct of the ritual, but also from the respective manners of father and daughter. He treated her as if she were a servant. She obliged, but when out of his line of sight, behaved unsubtly flirtatiously with us. We could only imagine what he might do if he thought we were encouraging her.

As the blessing of the wine concluded, *melech ha'olam borei p'ri hagafen,* we invented a pretext, thanked them profusely for their hospitality, and excused ourselves, happily rejoining the melodious jabber of Bombay.

## Hell Train

Orders. Always orders. *Get going. Stay put. Get going again. Don't ask questions. Do your bit.*

In due course, our next assignment came unheralded by prior notice: fifty airmen, including me, were orally directed to pack our gear and assemble for transport from the *Victoria Terminus*. Oddly, customary hard copy *Movement Orders* were not distributed, which meant – yet again – we had no idea where we might be headed.

At the rail station, we were greeted by an older Indian fellow looking every inch the venerable patriarch, with wizened features, a long flowing white beard, and a time-worn linen dhoti. He waved at us furiously while spouting repeatedly, in pidgin English, "*Sahibs*, you come with me!" We had no clue that he was to be the train's driver on our mystery trip, but they were well-matched. Both the steam engine and the antiquated carriages it pulled were fit for the British Museum. At best, we figured, the beast had been manufactured in the late 19th century. Car interiors looked like they'd been used for hauling cattle – and not properly cleaned for decades.

They stank, and we were not told how long we'd be cooped up inside the miserably filthy sties. Plain slatted wooden benches, crusted with decayed and decaying organic matter, were to serve as both seating and, as it became necessary, platforms for sleeping. Where the planks abutted one another, cracks were filled with insect carcasses and their droppings.

Little did we know then that the accommodation was to be our living quarters for weeks on end. No doubt not knowing was a good thing, as otherwise there might have been a mutiny of sorts.

As our "Train to Nowhere" chugged along for days without visible signs of progress, we came to believe that Grandfather Whitebeard hadn't the foggiest what he was doing to get us to wherever the hell we were supposed to be going. Repeatedly, when he'd stop at a depot to refuel and take on engine water, we would inquire, as best we could in broken pidgin English, "Where do we go? When will we finish with train? How long? How long?" Each time we would receive the same manic, maddening reply. "*Sahibs*," he'd screech, taking us to task with an impatient shake of the head, "*soon.*" How long is *soon* we'd insist. "Soon, soon, *soon!*" he'd shout, brandishing a crumpled sheet of paper bearing indecipherable Hindi script, twirling it in jerky elliptical arcs over his head at full extension of a long, scrawny arm.

And so it went, day after day, as we continued to ride the rails in supreme discomfort. We subsisted on field rations consisting of dry hardened biscuits, tinned cheese and fatty, high-calorie bully beef, a tea bag, and powdered milk. Hot water for brewing was extracted from the steam engine through a tap at the bottom. We'd run the liquid until the piping stream ran relatively clear of mineral grit and other foreign particles.

The journey brought a whole new, ugly dimension to the phrase 'traveling rough.' Though we dreamt of many things, we'd have gladly settled for a hot meal now and then. At least the *cha*, or the Englishman's proverbial cup-o'-tea, was, under given the circumstances, considered to be rather excellent. Granting free rein to the imagination and with disciplined denial of the other senses, my cuppa could have been the same beverage being enjoyed whilst chatting back home in the sublime haven of Celia's kitchen. Ah, if only.

We hungered desperately for signs of civilization. Suddenly, as if an apparition of oasis had risen from parched desert sands, we found ourselves chugging past a stretch of military encampments. We ordered Whitebeard to bring the train to a halt and allow us to investigate.

Our great good fortune was to have come upon one of two dozen of the Indian army's prized Sikh battalions, fiercely courageous warriors who'd achieved glory on diverse battlefields for the better part of a century. They treated us as comrades-in-arms, generously sharing one of the jewels of their slim rations: steaming plates of surprisingly savory grilled soya link sausages.

The respite was short-lived. "*Sahibs*, we go now!" *Yes, Grandfather, you clueless madman.*

We were in bad shape. Daytimes, the tropical heat soared in excess of one hundred degrees Fahrenheit. The only breeze was that generated by the movement of our train. We took turns sitting on the carriage steps, grateful for even the slightest relief from stifling, oxygen-depleted air, prickly skin, and clogged sinuses.

Nighttime was no picnic, either. Bugs. All manner of nasty winged vermin. Mosquitoes. Small flies. Big flies. *Hungry* flies. Filmy, porous mosquito netting provided minimal relief from attack – and often exacerbated our vulnerability when bloodthirsty predators made it through a seam or a hole and got trapped inside. *Ugh!* The very thought of it makes my skin crawl.

Cleanliness and proper sanitation preoccupied us as well. Lest one court the risk of incurring a dread, debilitating disease, one soon learns to tend to the body's natural needs and functions diligently, especially in an inhospitable environment.

Every time we stopped at a railway station, regardless of whatever facilities were available on the platform, we found ways to wash the filth from our bodies and uniform. That didn't take much doing, as stations and depots within the Indian rail system were situated at or near a dependable water supply, whether drawn from an adjacent river or tributary, or pumped from a wellhead drilled down into an aquifer.

I can see it now. Broad daylight. Center of the platform. Stripped to my birthday suit. Standing directly under a head-high mounted spigot, with my clothing splayed out around my feet. Making the most of my brief allotment of time and purification as the airman to follow me worked the pump handle up and down, up and down, up and down. *Thank you, mate.*

Another novelty was that of *al fresco* shitting. The 'toilets' were deeply dug-out holes in the ground. No throne. Not even the suggestion of one. To empty the bowels successfully – that is, to do so without soiling oneself or falling backwards into the fecal abyss – one had to squat at just the right angle, maintaining the proper degree of tension in the buttocks and calves, and then let loose.

With every passing day, our disgust and consternation grew. Interminably long stretches of nothingness were dotted with rudimentary villages, paddy fields, and farmlands. Oh, for the ability to contact a British military liaison or a government office somewhere, anywhere. We were *de facto* captives, all because of some idiot of an RAF administrator not doing his or her job, relying solely upon a non-English-speaking and apparently daft train driver to deliver us to a destination known only to Whitebeard – and perhaps not even he knew for certain. Where oh where were the damned *Movement Orders*?

We were hungry, exhausted, bored to high heaven, emotionally drained, and filthy to the extent that we swooned from our own stench. Freely and openly, we discussed mounting concerns regarding risks of illness and degradation of our combat readiness. We considering abandoning the *Train to Nowhere* and making our own way to an outpost where a competent authority might be reached.

As we came to the precipice of that act of self-determination, our ten-day odyssey entered its final act. The train emerged from a forested area and bridged the *Ganga*, a tributary of the *Ganges* in West Bengal. We had traversed the country west to east, covering in excess of two thousand non-linear kilometers. Rural villages ceded to small towns and then larger ones evidencing signs of industrialization and modernization. We sensed that we were penetrating the outskirts of a major city. With hisses and groans, the engine labored to ascend a challenging hillside grade, then gained speed as it traced a long, loping soft curve toward a horizon bristling with tall buildings, smokestacks, and – *what ho!* – aircraft.

The atmosphere was electric. We crowded the windows and carriage steps for better views of our impending deliverance. Our yearning and anticipation were such that the slowing of the train as it approached Calcutta's Dum Dum Airport rail station was painfully difficult to endure. *Hurry! Hurry! Hurry up and stop!*

## Deliverance

Dum Dum Airport. Deliverance at last. We could have kissed the ground. Alas, however, there was no time for such pagan expressions of gratitude. The powers-that-be had orders and assignments ready and waiting to issue immediately upon our arrival.

I was put to work in a hangar, dispatching freight hither and yon. After a while, I was told to take charge of processing overseas mail arriving at an Army-based post office for RAF personnel spread across the whole of India. Bags upon bags had to be sorted and rerouted by code, a routine which required the assistance of a cadre of other airmen. Communication from hearth and home also came in the form of a matrix – a metallic letterpress form used to print copies of Britain's *News of the World*. Though typically dated by the time the average soldier laid hands on it, the journal served to boost morale, imparting a sense of "we're all in this together."

When not on duty we received passes to explore Calcutta (Kolkata as of 2001). Orders, however, were that all personnel departing camp must do so only in pairs. The supercharged political atmosphere, fueled by Mahatma Gandhi's *Quit India Movement*, was such that the streets of the city were deemed unsafe for British servicemen.

Also according to orders, we were not to carry sidearms when venturing forth. That didn't stop me from protecting myself. My trusty dagger, good for cutting rope, paring fruit, or self-defense, was ever at the ready, sheathed in a scabbard attached to my belt. At night, that same dagger went to bed with me, tucked under a pillow.

At a minimum, I expected the mere sight of the blade to be a deterrent to mischief-makers, brigands, or hostile natives. Fat lot of good that did. One evening, as I returned to camp with a buddy, we took incoming fire. I heard and felt the rush of a bullet as it whizzed past my ear. Another fraction of an inch closer, and it would have found its mark: a head shot.

Close calls such as that can be quite scary. The what-ifs

consume the imagination. Still, it's far better than sustaining the first cousin of a close call: stopping the bullet with one's body. Charles de Gaulle survived many an assassination attempt. In 1962, the Citroen in which he was being driven sustained over one hundred ballistic strikes at the hands of OAS gunmen[14].

Not a one hit home. Afterwards, De Gaulle commented dryly, "Those gentlemen are poor shots." Apparently, my would-be assassin was one as well, thank goodness.

In its socioeconomic aspects, Calcutta was a carbon copy of Bombay, bearing the hallmarks of colonialism, caste, and custom. The privileged lived and worked in upscale districts booming with commerce. On foot and by rickshaw, bus, and motorcar, the well-off and the middle class luxuriated in the ambience of streets and tree-lined boulevards bordered by smart, modern buildings housing banks, offices, municipal and provincial courts, hotels, temples, retail shops, cinemas, clubs, and restaurants.

Therein, as well, was the *Old Opera House*, dating from the early 1800s, which had been converted in wartime to a theatre hall for the entertainment of Allied troops, and downtown's vast *Chowringhee Market*, where anything and everything was available and negotiable, even and especially for foreigners in uniform.

Then one might turn a corner or cross a track and enter another world, that of unremitting misery and degradation. As in Bombay, Calcutta's wretched and their children suffered mightily and openly in beggary and prostitution. The swift transition from protected enclaves exuding wealth and high station to unguarded slums reeling with abject poverty, disease, and crime was jolting to the senses and the psyche. Inhabitants of that grim world did not know of war. War was not on their doorstep. Their preeminent threat was environmental, that of dire and desperate conditions

---

[14] The *Organisation armée secrète* (OAS, or Secret Army Organization) was "determined to use all means necessary, including the most violent, to prevent the government of President Charles de Gaulle from granting Algeria independence." Source: <https://www.encyclopedia.com/>.

which rendered every day a battle for survival.

## A Tourist in Uniform

I made the most of my grants of leave by visiting, as if a tourist, several of the land's far-flung major cities, including New Delhi, some fifteen hundred kilometers northwest of Calcutta, and Hyderabad, an equal distance southwest. Twice, too, I was fortunate to be able to enjoy spells of *R-and-R* at encampments set in the formidably mountainous terrains surrounding Darjeeling and Shillong to the north and northeast.

Darjeeling was and is a renowned tealeaf-growing region, with a temperate climate perfect for producing some of the world's finest. Reaching the heady heights of Darjeeling, however, was an adventure, to put it mildly. Though we were young, relatively fearless, and occasionally recklessly daring, native drivers put our gung-ho mettle to the test.

It would be a misnomer and overstatement of the highest order to call what we traveled on 'roads.' They were at best glorified donkey trails, devoid of guardrails, replete with blind curves and vertiginous ascents. Our motormen attacked them with abandon, despite the inherent hazard of the sudden appearance of an oncoming vehicle coming around a bend barely wide enough, and sometimes less, to accommodate the passage of two. Our salvation was the region's vehicular gate system, timed to regulate traffic traveling in opposite directions along the more treacherous stretches. Plus, we prayed a lot.

Our brief sojourn in the cool mountain air, far, far away from *DROs*, wilting heat and humidity, and proximity to increasingly hostile anticolonial activism, was well worth the adventure.

## Mud and Guts, Bugs and Rot

The ruinous monsoon season runs from June through September, inundating low-lying fields, destroying crops, and disrupting lives. In anticipation of the annual deluge, we broke camp and moved to higher ground in a more desirable, sheltered location. Nevertheless, when the rains came, as they did with a vengeance, we eventually found ourselves knee-deep in thick, boot-sucking mud. And not just any old thick, boot-sucking mud. No, this particular gooey slime had a quality all of its own: that of foul corruption of the flesh. Did our leaders not know that they'd been directed to relocate our bivouac to the site of a former cemetery? That relentlessly penetrating rainwater would produce hydraulic upward seepage of the fluids of rotting corpses?

We lived and labored within the stench of death for months until we were able to move again

Local villagers were able to build out campsites in a matter of days. Bunkhouse framing, flooring, walls, roofing, and bedding – all of them were constructed of indigenous bamboo and its byproducts. Bamboo is an organic material with remarkable versatility in a wide variety of applications, and it seemed to grow everywhere. Shaved into strips and soaked in water for pliability, it could be plaited into sheets to make mattresses, thatched roofing, furniture seating foundations, and more.

Bedframes were inelegant four-posters designed to facilitate draping of mosquito netting. The winged vermin we encountered during the course of our *Train to Nowhere* misadventure were endemic during the monsoon season. The nasty things assaulted our flesh and hectored our sleep. Netting, as before, was a most imperfect barrier and deterrent. Before settling down for the night, we would be on our knees, acting like manic monkeys in trying to kill the critters by clapping them between open hands, squashing the bloody guts out of them, to reduce their legion before they began biting the hell out of us.

Absolutely necessary despite its limited reliability, netting frustrated not only the bloodsuckers but also, sadly, freshening breezes. Even should one be so lucky as to spend a whole night in bed without being prey to a single invader, stifling stale air and profuse sweating would bedevil one's sleep. Between that and drinking plenty of water to combat dehydration, the necessity to answer nature's call meant having to leave the gauzy cocoon and hasten to the outdoor latrines.

I will not further describe the experience. Suffice to say that to this day, when such moments come to me in a dream, they are the stuff of nightmares of revulsion.

The one and only luxury (if you could call it that) in which we indulged was that of taking advantage of the abundant supply of cheap local labor, everything from running errands to shining shoes and doing laundry. The latter, we discovered, came with a price tag of its own: that of the degree of cleanliness.

After a modicum of exertion and body sweat, supposedly freshly laundered undergarments, shirts, and trousers would emit vexingly nasty odors. We were forever giving the load bearers extra soap with which to wash our bundled attire, but the result seemed to be invariant. Why? We determined the root of the problem: ritual. Villagers were laundering our clothing as they had done their own for centuries, in streams and rivers that had long since become polluted through overuse and runoff.

Even at night, noxious aromas plagued us. Blankets woven from Indian wool responded to moist body heat by emitting the stench of rotting flesh. Again, why? British scientists readily isolated the problem: particles of sheep dermis embedded in the weave. It appeared that farmers, in their hasty efforts to extract greater amounts of wool at shearing time, had been yanking hanks of fibers from their charges, roots and all.


## Tedium, Tourism ... War

We knew, of course, that we had not been transported and posted, circuitously and at great expense, for the dubious pleasures of endurance training, casual tourism, and acculturation in the twilight of Britain's hold on India. War was literally on the horizon, due east, in Burma, where Allied forces had been battling the occupying Japanese, with little success, ever since the enemy had seized the territory in 1942.

Enter    Admiral    Louis    Mountbatten,    Supreme    Allied

Commander of *SEAC*, the *South East Asia Command*, formed in August of 1943, responsible for strategic planning and leadership of all theater forces land, sea, and air. He was to serve in that role until mid-1946, some nine months after V-J Day. Pursuant to newly issued orders, we would serve proudly under his command.

Much has been written by military historians regarding the ebb and flow of period warfare in Southeast Asia, from the onset of Japan's invasion of Burma to Allied forces' capture of Rangoon in May 1945 and mop-up operations thereafter. Such 'satellite' views are theirs to tell. My experiences, as related here, are representative of multitudinous operations performed on that grand scale – operations which, taken together, succeeded in winning the day.

### Chittagong and Beyond

The port city of Chittagong, situated at the northernmost apex of the Bay of Bengal three hundred fifty-seven kilometers east of Calcutta, was a critically important staging area for Allied flight operations. Our contingent, part of the RAF Third Tactical Air Force, provided all manner of ground support – airfield clearance and security, runway readiness, ordnance resupply, cargo handling, and aircraft maintenance and repair.

As intended under Mountbatten's command, combined and coordinated resources of the RAF and the U. S. Army Air Forces took the war to the enemy while also assuring delivery of critical fuel, materiel, prefabricated Bailey-bridge trusses, and foodstuffs to Allied warriors on the ground – principally, the multinational Commonwealth fighting force of the British Fourteenth Army.

Our propeller-driven charges comprised a motley assortment of awesome aircraft, including the Curtiss C-46 *Commando* and the Douglas C-47 Skytrain *Dakota* – obese, lumbering transports, workhorses of the campaign – and the Republic P-47 *Thunderbolt* fighter.

Conditions at frontline support positions were vastly different from those of well-established, uncontested territories in the rear. As our battle forces advanced, so too did specialized units, led by

British engineers, tasked with clearing long, broad stretches of jungly terrain in order to fashion landing strips and resupply stations. They worked round the clock with bulldozers, trucks, and heavy rolling equipment to prepare a welcome mat for the *Commandos* and *Dakotas*, our fully laden behemoths of the sky.

Ground crews, working tirelessly despite the inherent hazards of their occupations, were the unsung heroes of forward position operations. In addition to wilting heat and humidity, our bodies were under constant assault by deafening noise and high-velocity grit churned up by roaring engines and propeller blades. Ear baffles? Nose guards? Goggles? Never happened. Perhaps our commanding officer was unaware of the conditions under which we labored. Not once did I see him visit the airfields.

Our staging post featured some forty personnel, including the aforementioned commanding officer, an adjutant, a few NCOs, and a few so-called cooks. Also, in the performance of rote loading and unloading operations, we were aided by Indian military detailed to our squadron.

At any one time, several aircraft could be either approaching or circling the airfield, waiting their respective turns to land. Pressure to perform well and quickly was intense, but we were equal to it. Our turnaround time was remarkably expeditious. Pilots landing their aircraft learned to trust our flaggers, following their signals without question, taxiing to the nearest vacant bay where truck crews were at the ready to relieve cargo holds of their burdens. Adjacent to the receiving bays was the departure runway. As soon as the titans' bellies had been emptied, they would take off again. Provisioning cycles ran continuously until flight operations had ceased for the day.

American air crews, while awaiting completion of the unloading of their aircraft, typically lolled about, sitting in the shade of a wing, drinking beer and shooting craps, rattling the dice, blowing on them in their hands, shouting "Bring My Baby Back Home" as they tossed them onto a makeshift playing surface. I always got a kick out of that.

The Yanks fascinated me in many ways: Their accents and

vocabulary; their happy-go-lucky swagger; and the superior state of their amenities and technologies. G.I. tents were cleverly lined and ventilated, and not just those of the senior officers. Each man had a collapsible bed with a real mattress, a far cry from our lot: a four-man stretcher strapped to wooden poles hammered into the earth. Plus, portable field ovens had been shipped to their encampments so that they could enjoy a hot meal now and then. At one U.S. forces bivouac, I espied open-air tables heaping with freshly baked bread and go-withs. The aromas drove me nuts. I plead guilty to having asked one of my Indian aides to nick one for me!

Yankee crew members became familiar faces to us, making as many as three round trips per day in their zeal to accumulate as quickly as possible a sufficient number of sorties to qualify them for rotation back to the States.

With each advancement against the retreating enemy, we would pull up stakes and move forward to establish the next improvised airfield. American flight control personnel moved into position first, followed by the RAF. Tropical conditions continued to plague us, but we had learned how take care of ourselves and still get the job done fast and well – a testament to the spine and spirit of our SEAC brothers and sisters.

Apart from the relentless heat and humidity, our bodies were under assault as well by another endemic foe: ants. Mega-ants. Red ants so large that they had been known to chew through the soles and uppers of boots left on the ground. To thwart their nocturnal incursions, we would soak the posts of our bedframes in liquid paraffin or some such deterrent chemical brew, but nothing worked as effectively and satisfyingly as squishing their fat, crackly exoskeletons underfoot.

Once in setting up camp, I remember having offered my expertise in helping to set up protective overhead tenting for the open-sided cookhouse. As the first hot meal was being prepared, the chief cook commenced coughing. We had inadvertently omitted fashioning a hole in the peak of the roofing to allow smoke to escape. The man's fits of choking and gagging were so severe, we thought we had very nearly killed him – which, given his culinary aptitudes, would have been a service to King or Queen or whoever happened to be occupying the throne at the time. His meals were so wretched, he might just as well have been working for the enemy.

Our days were such that we could always bank on something unexpected happening – which certainly did keep things interesting. One particular incident stands out. In preparation for moving on to the next forward airfield position, another airman and I had been performing winding-up operations at our soon-to-be abandoned base of operations. The American flight control group had already packed their gear and broken camp.

Even so, we might have been able to handle the arrival of a jumbo – except for the fact that the arrivals runway had become hazardously inhospitable. Dead center in the airstrip, a massive pit had formed. We conjectured it might have been the site of a depleted, filled-in watering hole, and that repeated exposure to the shockwaves of heavily laden aircraft finally caused it to implode.

Our ears perked up as we discerned the unmistakable rumble of a C-47's engines, throttling back in anticipation of landing. There was no way the pilot would be able to spot the runway anomaly before he was committed to putting the *Dakota* on the ground. If one of the plane's wheels were to catch in the gap at touchdown speed of one hundred fifty miles per hour, then plane, crew, and cargo would be destroyed in the blink of an eye.

My workmate and I had to think fast. We were the only ones aware of the impending disaster, and we had no means with which to orally communicate with the pilot. The sole tool we had at our disposal, in the back of our Jeep, was an Aldis battery-powered signal lamp used for flashing Morse Code messages – and for beaming green light for *clearance* or red light for *stop*.

Our Jeep became 'flight control' as we sped to the perimeter of the sinkhole, hastily inserted a red filter into the Aldis lamp, mounted the contraption, and commenced signaling. *Go round! Go round! Go round!* our repetitive flashing commanded. The pilot acknowledged with a dip of a wing, gained airspeed, and aborted the landing. That, however, merely deferred the problem, as that plane simply *had* to get on the ground – and right soon.

Secure in our knowledge that the pilot would not attempt another landing on the arrivals runway, we raced to the departures strip, where another transport, a C-46 *Commando*, engines revving, was moments from taxiing to takeoff. *Cut engines!* we signaled. *Cut engines!* When it was safe to approach, we called out and explained the predicament. Immediately, via wireless transmitter, the *Commando* pilot apprised the *Dakota* of the situation and cleared the departures runway, thus enabling their fellow airmen to make landfall without incident.

After the dust had settled, we took the *Dakota* crew on a Jeep ride to the abominable abyss. Lusty rounds of profoundly grateful thanks and handshakes ensued. They were lucky to be alive. As were we, years into a war that had years yet to run.

All in a day's work.

## Currencies of Gratitude

To say that war is hell is a given and an all-too-casually tossed off platitude. War *is* hell, and within that hell, in my humble opinion, there is no more searing station than that occupied by the infantry. Furthermore, to wage that war against an implacable enemy within the bowels of a festering, stinking, inherently perilous jungle takes a special breed of soldier. The foot soldier.

There came a time when a unit of the Fourteenth Army arrived at our camp, hoping to fly out on a cargo-emptied transport the next day to begin their homeward journey. The men were drenched to the skin, shivering, famished, and thoroughly exhausted. They'd had only their rubberized cape groundsheets to protect them from monsoon downpours day after day, night after night.

As we were not a transit camp, we had no formal accommodations for them. They craved sustenance, dry clothing, and rest. Being British, of course, the first order of business for one and all was the brewing of stiff black cha, the Englishman's proper cup of tea, as we rustled up a meal for them, doing our best to make field rations as appetizing as possible. But where to bed them down?

We found space for some on and between our stretcher beds, but there were far too many to house in our canvas 'barracks.' Standing orders to the contrary, I stuck my neck out and led the remainder to the food storage mess tent. Ravenous men smack dab in the middle of our limited inventory of comestibles? I could almost hear my CO barking, "What the bloody hell were you thinking, Fersht?" What was I thinking? *Duty and honor*.

The following morning, I helped to set up seating for the unit in one of the departing *Dakotas*. Seating, such as it was, consisted of no more than metal-framed canvas sacks strapped to the sides of the fuselage. Running down the center were carefully weight-distributed items of baggage and gear, securely lashed down to prevent movement in flight. "Ready to board," I called out to the first knot of soldiers who'd begun to queue up.

Toward the rear of the line, one of the fellows whom I'd lodged in the mess tent hurried about amongst his brethren. At first it appeared to me that they were shaking hands or performing some sort of sign language. As that same soldier's turn came to board, he smiled at me and thrust his hands forward, each clutching fistfuls of cigarettes, currencies of comradeship and gratitude.

"This is for taking care of us last night," he said. As much as I attempted to graciously decline their expression of appreciation, they insisted. We'd done the best that we could do under the circumstances, but for them, it was everything. Trust, respect, and empathy. Each of them, in their own way, gave great thanks for our meager hospitality. "We get to go home now," one of them acknowledged with a tip of the cap, "while you blokes carry on in this godforsaken jungle."

I was so deeply touched by their deed, realizing their precious ration of cigarettes was most probably all they could offer me. Yet it was *we* who should have been thanking *them* – for serving bravely and stoically without complaint in the fiercest station of hell.

## Letters from Home

My dear sister Celia regularly mailed to me letters from home, which I'd receive weeks later in bundles. One of those letters bore some extremely sad news: one of my cousins, Alec Jacobs, had died making the supreme sacrifice for his country as a Japanese prison-of-war in Borneo. He had been the first in our family to be conscripted into service and, eventually, posted to the Southeast Asia theater.

All reports indicated that most of the prisoners held in Borneo had died of severe malnutrition. Those that were still alive as Fourteenth Army troops advanced into enemy territory during the late-stage Borneo campaign phase of 1945 had been put to death by the fleeing enemy. Freshly dug graves bore silent witness to the slaughter.

I was devastated. What could I do? What could I say? What information could I obtain to comfort his grieving parents? "Nothing," said my CO. "There's a war on."

## Endemic Enemies

Bombs, bullets, and bayonets kill. They were the manmade agents of death with which we coexisted every waking day. Climate, disease, and insidious forces of nature – they, too, exacted a horrendously significant toll on fighting ability and life.

Cholera and dysentery, malaria and prickly heat, dehydration, heatstroke, snakebite, parasites, vermin, you name it, we contended with it. Vigilance and common sense were paramount if one were to survive the onslaught of such pernicious assailants.

I recall that one of our flight mechanics lost his life due to what deductive forensic examination of the scene determined to be a tragic lapse. Poor Reggie had been so engrossed in what he was doing, servicing a plane engine, that as he leaned over the cowling to reach in, he failed to notice his pith helmet had slipped off his head. Either that, or he discounted the effect of relatively brief exposure to punishing sunrays. However long it was, the lack of protection was of sufficient duration to begin to bake his brain. When he passed out, the sun continued to wreak havoc. His inert body, with a ratchet wrench still gripped in one hand, was found face down below the nose of the aircraft. His headgear lay not far away, its chin strap unbuckled.

Another equally insidious hazard was that of imbibing tainted water. Potable supplies were like liquid gold. Retreating Japanese soldiers destroyed anything and everything left behind that might benefit their pursuers, including water sources. Contemptibly, they would poison wells by dumping rotting corpses into them.

All of our drinking water, regardless of source, was boiled prior to consumption. Despite such precaution, though, some fell ill to yellow jaundice – I among them. For days, I'd been lethargic, unable to muster an appetite and achy all over. I forced myself to down an occasional banana. Hot tea without milk kept me from dehydrating. I remember being slumped over, planted at a desk in the Squadron Orderly Room as my CO came through. He took one look and had me rushed to sick bay, where the on-duty medical officer confirmed the diagnosis: viral-borne *Hepatitis A*. In short order, prone on a stretcher, I was transported to a British military hospital in Imphal, some three hundred fifty kilometers northeast of Chittagong.

By the time I arrived at hospital, my simplistic acts of self-treatment had proven to be relatively successful, which, unfortunately, turned out *not* to be a good thing. With overt symptoms of the disease virtually absent from my outward appearance, the examining doctor must have deemed me to be akin to certain soldiers who were apt to fake an illness in order to earn respite from frontline duties. He classified me as a malingerer and had me promptly shipped, along with a bevy of other 'black sheep,' to a so-called convalescence camp. There, after a cursorily brief recuperation period, we were ordered to assemble for parade in full battle dress, with heavy boots, helmets, loaded backpacks – the works.

Amongst the twenty-five or so unlucky men selected for

discipline were four airmen, including me. Sadly, we stood out from the rest as our kit included regular shoes, white socks, khaki shorts, powder blue open-neck shirts, and royal blue forage caps.

A sergeant-major strode forward, regarding us with sneering disbelief, as if we Martians had had the temerity to land on *his* Planet Earth without permission. He circled us once, returned to the spot where he'd first encountered us, and went ballistic. "You're a disgrace to your uniform! A disgrace to the empire!" And those were the nice things he said compared to the torrent of invective and expletives that followed. After he'd fully vented his spleen, he ordered us to the quartermaster stores to be re-equipped in standard British Army issue for another nasty parade session after lunch.

Before we airmen reported to the quartermaster, we discussed our plight. Happily, one of our quartet was himself an NCO in the RAF quartermasters cadre. "Leave the talking to me," he advised – and of course, we did.

It was a classic case of equality of peers, quartermaster to quartermaster. Our man pointed out to his British Army opposite number that we were responsible for our own kit and nothing else. Each of us carried documents certifying that obligation.

Stymied, the Army man fumed and flexed his authority, snapping, "No equipment leaves here without a signature pledging responsibility for return in good order. You go tell that sergeant-major to *go fly a kite!*" (The expression he used was actually one heck of a lot pithier than that, but because my grandchildren and great-grandchildren will be reading this account one day, I've made a judicious substitution.)

Now we were caught between the proverbial rock and a hard place. We were in no hurry to return to face the intemperate sergeant-major. We walked about. The facility impressed us as more of a labor camp than a nursing-to-health station. We spotted soldiers slaving away digging trenches in the killer sun, allegedly to provide them with the recuperative powers of rugged exercise. To a man, we pined for the liberties granted us as frontline RAF support personnel. Finding a way, *any way,* to rejoin our squadrons became priority number one.

If we hadn't smartened up, there was a high likelihood the military police would have hauled us into the slammer. The very next morning, I stood in front of the hospital camp CO to inform him that I had neither the desire nor intention to 'convalesce' any further, that I was fully prepared to return to my unit and get back into the thick of it. *For God and Country ... Sir!* To the best of my knowledge, my three blue-cap companions may have done likewise.

We were granted our requests. After I'd made it back to my unit, our squadron CO – the very same decent fellow who had charitably seen to my hospitalization – asked me why I'd turned down a good long spell of convalescent treatment. My frank and earnest explanation won the day. He cut orders for me to enjoy a week's furlough in the cool, cleansing mountain airs of Shillong. Amen to that!

## The Enemy Within

Well into my six months of service in Burma, a new member joined our Squadron 38 Staging Post: Corporal Tyler Monroe. We hit it off immediately, and in short order we came to regard one another as friends. Imagine my surprise then, when one day soon after he'd gotten the lay of the land, he approached me a bit circumspectly, looking about to see if anyone else might be within earshot, and asked flatly, "Sidney, you're a Jew. Am I right?"

"Yes, so what about it?" I replied, my tone both defensive and challenging.

"It's not me," he hastened to make clear. "It's the CO's adjutant, Flying Officer Shelly. He doesn't like Jews. Just thought I should tell you."

I was stunned. It was happening again. The specter of the enemy within. A fury began to mount inside my head and heart, but I kept my powder dry. I sensed there was more. Monroe could tell I was waiting to hear the rest.

He continued. "Shelly held a meeting in his office with the NCOs. He told them outright that he doesn't like Jews. He said, 'There's one in our unit. Watch him.'"

*Watch him.* I could not believe what I was hearing. This was not Arbroath boot camp, where the Wing Commander instructed, "All Jews and others not of the faith fall out and face the brick wall." To me, this was far worse. An active Jew-hater in the ranks, in a position of authority no less, in the midst of a shooting war here in bloody ugly Burma, with pestilence and death all around – *a shooting war*, where the code of conduct and honor and duty demand that each soldier has another's back.

To my face, F/O Shelly had always presented himself as a regular guy. Soon after he'd received his commission, he'd picked me to serve as a clerical assistant in the headquarters office, typing and alphabetizing papers and files. Not once did I suspect he harbored feelings of antipathy toward people of my faith. Yet now the awful revelation: F/O Shelly, given to baseless fear and loathing, that enemy within, had made me the victim of his furtive malevolence by painting a target on my back.

I wanted to lash out at him. To accuse him of being who and what he was, a mindless Jew-hater, and as such, inherently disloyal to Flag and Country. I wanted to see him swing for treason. But who was I kidding? The man had friends. Powerful friends. They'd close ranks for sure.

I went wild with rage. I flew back to my tent, tore off my service-issued eyeglasses, and smashed them to pieces underfoot. My gratification was short-lived. *Great job, Sidney. Now you're blind as a bat.*

The very next morning, I was obliged to report to F/O Shelly, of all people, in order to request transport to Sick Quarters RAF HQ Imphal so that I could be outfitted with new spectacles. With some difficulty, I managed to maintain my composure and poker face. "Only the one pair, you see, Sir." I have zero doubt he suspected I was lying. He tried to put me off by claiming that there were no flights available, but I knew better, and in the end he couldn't bar me from doing what needed to be done.

At Imphal, I was examined by a Medical Officer whose last name I recall, but regrettably only that: Gordon. I explained that I'd had an accident and needed new glasses. Whilst examining my eyes, he asked me how long I had served at the front in Southeast Asia. I replied something like, "Far too long, Sir. More than two years." I commented pensively on my state of exhaustion. "Sometimes, Sir, I confess, I begin to doubt I'll ever make it home." Yes, I was lean to the threshold of emaciation, without a scintilla of body fat, but it was so unlike me to think or feel that way, not to mention giving voice to such dark musings.

That was about the extent of our conversation, and I never gave it another thought.

In due course, after having been outfitted so that I could see again, I returned to my unit, full of anxiety about how I was going to be able to handle my 'Shelly problem.' I had bought some time with my impetuous act, but I was back to square one.

Miraculously, a few weeks later, the hand of fate intervened to save the day. Out of the blue, orders arrived for Leading Aircraftman Sidney Fersht to be posted to RAF Staging Post 56, Santa Cruz, Bombay. *Bombay!* Way, way back in civilization. Hot meals. Decent bedding. *People.* It was a plum assignment, a gift of the gods – or was it?

I remember thinking that I'd have given anything to be a fly on wall in Adjutant Shelly's office, just to see the look on his snide puss as he read my transfer orders. Would he make a connection between my recent trip to Imphal and the stroke of good fortune that had come my way?

That got me to pondering along the same lines. Could it be that Dr. Gordon, the medical officer who had inquired gently of my service and condition, had himself set the wheels in motion? Was he of the faith? Or was he, quite simply and marvelously, a benevolent, caring individual who empathized with my plight and took matters into his own hands?

Either way, the fine man was a savior, and had I known in advance of his innate goodwill, I would have smashed my glasses one heck of a lot sooner!

## Santa Cruz, Bombay

Upon my arrival, I was told to report to the Squadron CO immediately. Most unusual for a lowly airman. *What have I done now*, I wondered?

I knocked, entered the CO's office, stood smartly at attention, and raised my outstretched right hand in a circular motion to hold against my temple, exactly twenty millimeters behind the eye. "Airman Fersht, Sir. Reporting for duty."

"Sheldon Boothsby," he replied, returning my salute. "Welcome."

Boothsby motioned for me to stand at ease and commenced to asking questions. What kind of work had I been doing? What was happening in the forward areas? How far had the Fourteenth Army advanced in Burma?

I briefed him as best I could. He seemed satisfied. Next, half hesitatingly, he fingered several files and papers splayed out on his desk. "These are your personnel records, Airman." After a long moment of awkward silence, during which he stared straight at me, he lifted a document off his desk and continued. "I'm wondering why there's a line scrawled across the one page stating, '*This airman has a biased opinion of the RAF*.' That doesn't seem to jibe with the rest of the package, nor with what you've just told me about your experiences. So what gives?"

Boothsby surely noticed the shocked expression on my face. "Sir, I haven't the slightest idea what that could be about. None whatsoever."

But I did have an idea: Shelly. The bastard Shelly, getting a screw-you, anti-Semitic lick in because I'd managed to escape the ambit of his ill-will.

Perhaps Boothsby appreciated the fact that I hadn't resorted to naming names. Or that he could see for himself that I had served the RAF and my country faithfully and well. Or both. In any event, before he dismissed me, another miracle: he promoted me to Acting Corporal *and* Acting Sergeant. Two successive promotions at the same time!

My elevations in rank probably had less to do with any specific acts or aptitudes evident in my records than they did with length-of-service and the nature of my new assignment: helping to sort out 'redundant' air crews, virtually all of whom were senior NCOs. Happily for them and what it said about the progress of the war, there were many. V-E Day was in the history books and ever-dwindling Japanese forces were being beaten back aggressively in Southeast Asia.

The crewmen whom I helped to sort out treated me like a *mensch*. They knew that I had served on the frontlines for years, and that as a staging post stalwart, I had been integral to the successful execution of their missions.

The new stripes on my sleeve entitled me to use of a Jeep. One of the first things I did after having settled in was to put in for a long overdue extended furlough – and I didn't have to travel far to become a beach bum. Magnificent Juhu Beach, a six-kilometer stretch of lustrous silken sands and balmy breezes hugging the eastern rim of the vast Arabian Sea, was minutes away.

### Tragedy in Paradise

Sensing that any day might bring a cessation of hostilities and orders to return to England, we had allowed ourselves to feel safe and secure. We had earned respite from bearing the unspoken, ever-present frontlines burden of knowing that tomorrow was a promise made to none of us. We had done our bit.

Juhu Beach. Clear, sunny skies and happy sounds of splashing, chatting, and laughter up and down the strand. A military policeman and I stood conversing about who-knows-what when both of us heard the droning growls of angry engines and explosive splats of rapid machinegun fire. *Zeros*! Japanese fighter planes roaring in and flying by at low altitude.

*Where the hell did they come from?* No time to think about that. In one syncopated movement, I leaped into the pillion seat of the MP's motorcycle as he straddled it and tore off. The wheels of the bike spewed arcing sprays of sand in our furious wake. Then, as we hit the bumpy, sunbaked surfaces of the upper beach, we nearly flew from our seats. We hugged that machine for dear life as we sped on, desperate to avoid being strafed.

When at last we became satisfied we'd escaped the immediate peril, we proceeded to the site where the *Zeros* had exacted their toll. I had come of age during the Battle of Britain. I had bicycled through bombed-out neighborhoods the morning after. I had seen death in its many guises. But I was unprepared for witnessing the carnage wrought by the enemy's final, futile attempts to turn the tide of the war.

Somehow, the Japanese had become aware of the construction of a new airstrip a short distance inland from the beach. Their mission was to halt its progress. It was a lightning attack, wholly unexpected. Scores of Indian laborers, manually laying and leveling beds of concrete, had been killed in place where they had been working. One fellow appeared to be resting, his arms holding fast to the sides of a concrete mixer, his head dipped down out of sight. My 'driver,' the MP, went to help him up and took hold of a shoulder, pulling him backwards. The man's corpse rolled and keeled over, revealing an eviscerated torso.

Hundreds of kilometers to the east, the British Fourteenth Army was advancing inexorably against the retreating Japanese. Yet here we were, betrayed by illusions of paradise and very much still in the firing line.

*When will it all end?*


### 'It's time for me to go home'

There's an old saying – Don't Look a Gift Horse in the Mouth – which has its origins in the legend of the *Trojan Horse*, a tribute delivered to the citizens of Troy containing, in the belly of the beast, units of the enemy Greek army.

My RAF Staging Post 56 Squadron CO had beknighted me with two instant promotions, to corporal and sergeant – but alas – there were significant strings attached. According to the *King's Regulations* of the Air Ministry, an airman was obligated to serve at least three months in uniform for each grade if those elevations were to become part of the permanent record.

I was on the threshold of being repatriated to the U.K. I had been in uniform in excess of five years, having served roughly half that time in frontline positions. I had escaped death by a whisker when a bullet whizzed past my head in Calcutta. I had dodged raining death at Juhu Beach. Nominally, neither venue had been considered a hot zone, but both incidents had been potentially lethal. Six more months? It was my call. I was not obligated to soldier on. "I would like to return home, Sir. Thank you, but no."

I was so hungry for home and country, for family and friends, for Celia and Kitty and all the others, I could almost taste it. Nostalgia began to set in. I found myself venturing frequently into Bombay, strolling along the docks where troop carriers and other larger-size vessels were leaving daily for Europe. For *Greenwich Mean Time*. One day as I sat on a bench, gazing longingly out to sea, daydreaming of the white cliffs of Dover, a young Indian lad approached me. "Shoeshine, Sahib?" he asked, unslinging a makeshift stand strapped over his shoulder.

"Yes," said I, placing my left foot on the working end of the box.

We chatted as he cleaned and polished. "What school do you go to?" I inquired, having randomly come up with a standard, child-relevant question out of the air.

"I go to the *cheder*, Sahib," he answered proudly. "The Jewish school."

The sceptic in me immediately raised the scam alert. Was he working me? Trying to ingratiate himself? Angling for a big tip? Had he been able to tell that I was Jewish, and if so, how? Was there something about me that was a giveaway? A tell? What were the chances?

I played along and put him to the test. "Good for you, young man. Let me hear you recite the Hebrew alphabet." That would fix him. I *had* him, surely.

Surely *not*. He proceeded to rattle it off: "*Aleph, beyt, gimal, dalet…*" The boy was the real deal. An Indian youngster of the Jewish faith after all. *Blimey.* After he'd finished, I tipped him handsomely, in good measure to atone for my unbecoming prejudgment.

Two days later, as I ambled along the same dockside stretch, I was beset by a mob of children chanting gleefully, "Sa-*hib*! Sa-*hib*! Sa-*hib*!" My authentically Jewish shoeshine boy had brought with him his entire Hebrew class. Lucky for me – and for them – my trouser pockets were fairly laden with *bucksheesh*, small denomination coins of gratitude.

### 'Will today be the day?'

Each morning, as soon as the daily orders were posted, I'd be there to check out the board on which they were posted. My excitement mounted with each sunrise. *Will today be the day?*

One day it was, in glorious black-and-white: last name F-E-R-S-H-T; first name S-I-D-N-E-Y.

Once again, Squadron CO Sheldon Boothsby called me into his office to dangle carrots. "Stay a while longer, Sidney, and you'll return home with the rank of Sergeant. You'd be in line for further promotion. Flight Sergeant. And who knows? A commission, maybe." Greater glory. Visions of sugarplums. The whole nine yards.

And once again, I declined straightaway: "No, thank you, Sir." Four unadorned one-syllable words that, strung together and spoken from the heart, said, "I elect to return home. I'm grateful for everything you've done for me. And I salute you."

Whether or not he suspected I'd opt to be repatriated, he was prepared with the ensuing question. "How would you like to get there? Plane or ship? Plane, you take a small kit bag and ship the rest of your gear home in a trunk."

"A plane, by all means!" I was floating on air.

And very soon thereafter, there I was: strapped in with seven other blokes in forward bomb bay of a Consolidated B-24 *Liberator*, with each of us having been issued a thick woolen blanket and a fistful of candy for sustenance during flight. Those two accouterments alone should have told us what was in store – a long, frigid journey, squeezed together in cramped quarters underneath the main deck of the fuselage. The four-engine, slab-sided giant had earned a well-deserved nickname: the *Flying Boxcar*.

If you needed to go to the bathroom, you had to clamber over the knees of the other passengers, then ascend to the next level behind the cockpit compartment to do your business. Our minimalist accommodations were not untypical of demobilization hospitality. *You want to get home fast? Be prepared to travel as second-class cargo where the sun don't shine.*

## The Waystation

We landed for refueling at Lydda Airport, southeast of Tel Aviv, in the British Palestine Mandate. Whom of all people did I run into there? None other than Sonny Ribbler. We hadn't seen one another in three years, and yet it seemed like only one yesterday once we got to talking.

We were transported together by truck to an army barracks for an overnight stay. We sat in the rear, looking back at the roadways, vehicles, buildings, and people as they came into view. Street signs in Hebrew struck a chord. *Mir bist heim*, we intoned in Yiddish. *We are home.* Yet we were not. England was some three thousand five hundred kilometers northwest, and Palestine was anything but the long-sought-after Jewish homeland.

We spotted British military occupying officers marching about, swagger sticks tucked under their arms, strutting with the bearing of colonial overlords. I became self-conscious of my uniform. My loyalties were being strained.

Our *Liberator*'s route had one more refueling stop to make. Rome. And thence to the golden shores of Albion and home sweet home.

## A Channel Crossing

When the *Liberator* had crossed the channel and cleared the coast of southern England, one of the crew popped down to announce the good news. We cheered. *Almost there.* We were exhausted – and exhilarated. But not yet home. Shortly thereafter, the aircraft banked and commenced its final approach. We heard and felt the rumbling of landing gear being deployed as the big bird descended and lined up with the runway. *Almost there.* When the underwing and nose wheels smacked down in succession with a reassuring *galump-galump* and a clean landing, we cheered again with uninhibited gusto. *England!* As the B-24 taxied to its assigned berth, we became animated, unbuckled our straps, and congratulated ourselves for having come full circle. We savored the moment deeply and piously as comrades-in-arms. Yet, technically, we were not yet home. Only after we'd deplaned and put our feet on British soil did our hearts swell to bursting. *Home again at long, long last!*

There was snow on the ground. Thick, white, fluffy stuff. The stuff of dreams. It had been years since any of us had seen such bounty of nature. Straight from roasting under a steaming hot tropical sun, we had been delivered to a winter wonderland.

We trudged through knee-deep crystalline drifts and made our way to a nearby camp for processing and paperwork. There was no fanfare. No huzzahs from celebratory onlookers. Only the company of one another, survivors all, greeted by cold wind and crunchy ice. We had made it. We were alive and well. We could not have asked for more.

A massive undertaking was well underway: transitioning the Crown's warriors from wartime footing to peacetime service – and thence, for the great majority, back into the mainstream of civilian life. Spread across the land were no less than seven disembarkation camps and nine dispersal units. I had arrived at Shorncliffe, a relatively isolated spot on the southeast coast, overlooking the Strait of Dover.

The first thing I remember doing after stowing my gear was calling home. The sheer joy and excitement radiant in my sisters' voices resonates in my ears today as it did then, more than sixty-two years ago: "It's our dear Sidney! Back home in England! Safe and sound!"

## The Airman at the Rail

All I needed to get from *Point A* Shorncliffe to *Point B* London, from yet another barren, tented barracks to the sweet embrace of family and friends, to bask in the glow of their sunny countenances and warm hearts, were new orders and travel vouchers.

What was I thinking as I awaited, patiently, the laboriously slow, creaky turning of the wheels of military bureaucracy?

I had volunteered to put myself in harm's way. The nation and our way of life had been subject to relentless attack by a murderous foe hellbent on world domination. To have done nothing would have been to risk everything. Thus, I had enlisted.

I found my thoughts returning to that introspective fellow standing at the rail of the *Stirling Castle*, lost in reverie in the midst of the vast Atlantic. It was as if I had recorded the scene from afar. Young Sidney Fersht, the newly minted airman, amidships on the starboard side, gazing into the gloaming as the vessel plowed forward, surrounded by an infinite expanse. Young Sidney Fersht contemplating the wholly unknowable.

Wind-driven chop blanketed the surface of the ocean as far as the eye could see. Within its sinister black depths, U-Boats were on the prowl, hunting for prey. I did not fear them. A boyish spirit of adventure carried me forward, relegating apprehensions of danger to the lower echelons of awareness of self.

I knew not what the future had in store for me. Though I would travel paths of war along with thousands, tens and hundreds of thousands of others, I had felt very much alone.

Between that singular moment and my safe-and-sound return to a much-changed country, I had experienced enough of life in its myriad manifestations to last a lifetime.

What might come next?

## Coming Home

Those creaky wheels finally turned in my favor. Furlough papers and travel voucher in hand, kit bag slung over my shoulder, I was advised that the weather in London was no better than that socking in the southern coast – drenching rain and cold to the bone. I didn't care one whit. I was heading home to see my family!

I had arranged to meet sisters Hettie and Freda at their place of business, a women's fashion emporium on the 'high street,' Kingsland Road, within the Hackney borough of North London. Sopping wet from head to toe, I entered to the *ding* of an overhead shopkeeper's bell and beamed with delight as they rushed forward to give me hugs and kisses, wet clothing and all.

Bless them, they had piping hot soup simmering on a small burner in the back. They were fairly *kvelling*, as the Yiddish expression goes – overflowingly joyful and exuberant, watching my every movement, as if I were an apparition of myself.

My heart swelled as well. The sensation of actually *being* home was beginning to blossom, and what an awesomely wonderful feeling that was.

Amidst these expressions of sheer excitement and glee, a customer popped into the store. The first words out of her mouth were, "Goodness, it smells good in here!"

Hettie and Freda greeted her warmly and introduced her at once to their youngest sibling, now an object of bragging rights, and rightly so. "Meet Sidney, our baby brother in the RAF, home at last. Just back from India after all these years." All my life I had been the 'baby brother,' and regardless of the passage of time, the paths I had traveled, and the deeds I had done, I would remain so, with abiding affection.

Hettie proceeded to telephone Celia, in Leicester, and the rest of those siblings who could be reached. "He's here! Our Sidney is home!"

Freda offered to shepherd me to her home, where I could avail myself of a warm bath, dry clothing, a full meal – and an afternoon kip, should I wish. It was then that it became incumbent on her to share with me the sad news she had theretofore spared me: her husband, Morrie, had succumbed to a massive coronary whilst I was overseas, leaving her to raise two young children as a single parent. But not all on her own. She had family. *Our* family.

A prime example of such devotion and generosity was Freda's offer to have me stay with her and the children whilst the powers-that-be determined where and when my last lap of service would be set forth. "We'd be happy to have you, Sidney," she said, "until you get things sorted out."

Brother Joe was the only other member of my immediate family who had served in uniform during the war. He and I bonded immediately, naturally, as no one who has not engaged in such conflict can truly appreciate and relate to its enduring impact on perspective and bearing.

The others, and I do not fault them for this, could only see me as the young lad who had left their company to fight the good fight. From their fixed frame of reference, although my jacket sported battle ribbons and my face had visibly aged, 'baby brother' had come home. Time had stood still. We had little in common except for childhood memories, and thus, though I loved them with all my heart, I found it difficult to relate to them.

Had they outgrown me—or had I outgrown them?

## Still in Uniform

Within a few days, I had hit the road, so to speak, making rounds within London and traveling widely to adjacent and nearby counties to reunite with far-flung family and friends. I soaked up every ounce of their revitalizing kindness, warmth, and affection.

It was an odd feeling, though, experiencing such freedom of movement. Sleeping late. Knowing that I didn't have to report to someone somewhere – at least not straightaway. Of course, I had enjoyed many a furlough during the war years, but these liberties were different in a profoundly significant aspect: there would be no returning afterwards to a forward bivouac. No standing in the line of fire.

Alas, it wasn't very long before new orders did arrive for me in the post. I was to report to an RAF unit based in Sutton Coldfield, a town in Birmingham, West Midlands, some two hundred kilometers northwest. Even though the posting would be of short duration, I considered myself most fortunate. Celia and her family lived about an hour's drive east in Leicester, and in Birmingham itself cousin Chunny, my mother's eldest brother's son, had a home.

Chunny's mum, like my own, had passed away when he was young. He practically grew up in our home, and being the same age as Celia, the two of them had bonded as brother and sister.

Chunny and spouse Gert welcomed me and treated me enthusiastically from the moment I appeared on their doorstep. They accorded me the status of a potentate making a state visit. Their happy eyes spoke volumes. "Just look at him!"

Chunny went on and on about my uniform and service to country. He insisted I take his favorite armchair. "What can we get for you, Shmeeloo? Ask for anything, and it's yours." *Shmeeloo.* My childhood nickname. I hadn't been called that in eons. Baby Brother was I once again – and happily so. I can still picture the love beaming from his face. He made me feel ten feet tall.

## Sutton Coldfield

My new (and thankfully ultra-short-term) posting turned out to be quite interesting. A large warehouse-like building housed a combination science laboratory, testing facility, and shipping hub – from which all manner of exotic equipment and instruments were being dispatched across the commonwealth.

On one floor, titled the *Experimental Station*, glass objects were packed into containers of varying shape, size, construction, and interior fill. The containers were then dropped to the ground from progressively higher altitudes to determine their relatively efficacy in preventing breakage during the course of transit.

My mates and I, all ex-flight crew and support personnel, had been assigned to serve there not because we had any particular aptitude for the scientific work being conducted, but rather because we were warm bodies who, while awaiting demobilization orders, could be put to good use as manual laborers. I had been lumped in with the NCOs, thankfully, because my double-boosted rank had not yet been rescinded.

*All hail the DROs!* The day did come, and right soon, when the posted *Daily Routine Orders* listed my name. I was about to obey the RAF high command for the very last time in uniform, following their instructions to accept an honorable discharge, proceed to the discharge depot, shuffle through the paperwork bureaucracy, collect a complete change of civilian clothing, and walk out the door with no strings attached. *Selah!*

*Civilian clothing.* Haberdasher, anyone? No. Not by a longshot. Oh, there were plenty of dry goods from which to choose. Racks upon racks of tweed suits of varying sizes, but otherwise woefully identical: the cheapest of fabrics, badly tailored, single-breasted. Plus, oceans of the dregs of shoes, shirts, and underwear. To tote one's newly acquired wardrobe, we were provided with a large cardboard box featuring a twine-and-wood parcel handle.

The mustering-out ceremony consisted of the quartermaster clerk bellowing sportingly, "On your way, civilians!" And that was that. At least I was leaving the service with more than when I came in. A ridiculous cardboard box containing an even more ridiculous outfit. Discharge papers – *yes!* A travel warrant. And my final pay – which included a lump-sum severance sufficient to treat myself to a ploughman's lunch and a pint of porter at the *Pig & Whistle*.

Nevertheless, we exited the building relieved and upbeat, and made our way on foot to the local railway station. I had the distinct feeling we must have looked like a bunch of penguins or costumed chorus boys, each carting identical, crude pieces of luggage by their goofy string handles. Doubtless we were a familiar sight to townspeople who lived and worked in the area. They knew from whence we came and that we were about to join their civilian ranks. Their hand waves and admiring smiles said, "Well done … and God bless."

## What to Do?

No longer employed as Leading Aircraftman Sidney Fersht, I would now be obligated to seek work as a member of the country's hungry-for-work labor force. Though there were many municipal and governmental positions favoring the recently ex-military, some of which might have been suitable to my experience and temperament, I worried that my abysmal elementary school record and relatively low rank in the RAF would hold me back from any reasonable likelihood of advancement. I'd been carrying the actual and psychic baggage of a failed education for years. While it had zero effect on my wartime service, the prospect of being held to account for it now concerned me greatly.

I could have applied for and secured employment as an airline industry traffic officer, but what kind of future would there have been in that? Plus, I'd had a bellyful of pompous ass stuffed shirts of the upper crust lording it over the hardscrabble hoi polloi, of which I was a member in good standing.

No. No form of government service appealed to me at that point. I had graduated from the school of hard knocks. I had served and served well for King, Queen, and Country. It was time for me to resume the role of Private Citizen and make my own way.

Make my own way. But where and how? And by what means to make the adjustment? The wartime military had their own fast-track timetable: six short weeks from undisciplined street kid to close-order-marching fighting machine. Then six long years in uniform, being told where to go, what to do, and when to do it, dawn to dusk, day in and day out. Six formative, young adult years of being fed, clothed, housed, armed, ordered into battle, surviving or dying.

Then suddenly, with the stroke of a pen, a cardboard box and a parting salute: "On your way, civilians!" The abrupt separation from what had felt like forever spent in the meat grinder of global conflict was like awakening startled, cold, and damp from a deep dream state – or a nightmare – into a stark, unfamiliar reality.

Yet, I was undaunted by any of it. I'd made my own way before and would do so again. If wartime service had taught me anything, it was that a certain hackneyed adage applied with utter and apt validity: When the Going Gets Tough, the Tough Get Going.


## A Family Business

During the war years, Kitty had lived in Leicester with Celia's family. There, she met and married a fine fellow, Joe Gabriel, who had been turned down for military service because of a non-life-threatening medical condition. Joe, who managed the local branch office of the Bellow Machine Company, knew I was not particularly looking forward to reentering the tailoring trades. He offered me a job in a related capacity: that of repairing sewing machines, of which his firm was a leading distributor of original equipment and replacement parts. With no other prospects on the horizon, I asked myself, "*What do you have to lose? Why not give it a go?*"

The answer was *yes*. "Thank you, Joe. I'm in." With that, I donned a pair of overalls and set about learning sewing machine mechanics. Within two days, I had 'graduated' to repairman and was sent out, all on my own, to service the company's widespread industrial customer base. Those garment factories which did not have a fulltime mechanic onboard needed periodic visits from 'experts' such as I, because employees being paid piece-rate for their production took little if any time to perform basic maintenance – relatively simple cleaning and lubrication functions that, if not done on a regular basis, gum up the works and risk damaging critical parts.

Most of the time, all I needed to do was extract accumulated thread and fluff wrapped around or adhering to moving parts; oil the machine; tighten a screw here and there; insert a fresh needle – and *voilà*! Working fine again. Most of the time. To deal with those occasions when routine maintenance and intuitively comprehensible fixes did not result in success, I had been instructed to play a waiting game – to select a part at random, declare it unfit, take it with me – ostensibly to be replaced – and then turn the matter over to a more experienced machinist who would return to diagnose and address the non-functioning unit.

Joe was a consummate salesman. He spent the majority of his time traveling throughout the Midlands, courting new customers while also making sure that existing clients were happy with Bellow. Occasionally, he would invite me to go along with him as a learning experience. I appreciated his thoughtfulness, of course, as it portended opportunity for advancement.

All was going well until one day, without any symptoms to indicate incipient illness, I doubled over, wracked by severe stomach pain and nausea. Somehow, I made my way to Kitty's place on Cambridge Street. She took one look at me, got me into bed, and phoned the doctor. By the time he made his house call the next morning, I was in bad shape. His bedside manner was not pretty. "Bloody hell!!. Why didn't you get yourself to hospital straight off, Sidney?!" he barked. I was chastened, and Kitty felt badly, too. At Leicester Infirmary Hospital, they made the doctor's diagnosis official: acute appendicitis – with first stage peritonitis setting in.

I was lucky. I'd dodged yet another bullet. While recuperating, I contemplated paths taken, paths not taken, and the road ahead.

Did I see myself making a career of sewing machine sales and service, in the Midlands or anywhere else? No, not really.

With great thanks to Joe for having provided the shelter and security of a regular paycheck so soon after my employment as a soldier had ended, I returned to London. Freda again graciously offered to put me up in a spare room until such time as I became settled and ready to be on my own. "You'll be good company for the children, too." What a dear.

"What kind of occupations am I qualified or suited for?" I asked myself, taking inventory. Hunting and killing Japanese infantry, yes – but there was no need for that anymore. Repairing sewing machines – I'd opted *not* to do that anymore. Delivering furniture or scouring gluepots – ancient history. Tailoring – not nearly a frontrunner, given memories of childhood exploitation, but clearly the one line of work best substantiated by my thin résumé.

Having no viable alternatives, I decided to give it another go and soon found work with a prestigious women's clothing manufacturer located in the fashionable West End. What can I say? After all those years away from the business, I still had a knack for it. Rock of eye. Sure, steady hands. Confidence at the cutting table. In short order, I was earning good money, able to pay my own way, feeling like a *mensch*.

The city had changed so that walking its streets produced an odd sensation of being unmoored, of being out of place and time. I'd happen upon wide open spaces where commercial and residential buildings and iconic landmarks had once stood. Absent, too, were family members who had been driven from the East End by the *Luftwaffe* and by Wernher von Braun's indiscriminate shower of lethal V-2 rocket bombs. They had not yet returned. The few friends that I had before the war were gone from the old neighborhood as well – never to be seen or heard from again. So much of the context of my teenage youth had been either expunged or displaced by war. In a manner of speaking, I had become orphaned again.

## Life Goes On

Outwardly, I had settled. I'd found employment. I was earning a decent wage. I had converted from soldier to ordinary working stiff. Inwardly, I remained restless and searching. From the age of fourteen, after I had been orphaned literally through the death of my parents and then sped by the prevailing winds of class custom into the labor force, I had not been one to passively accept that my lot was fated. There had to be more to living life than making a meal of whatever was dished on one's plate. There had to be, and it was up to me to make that happen.

In making my way, I managed to locate second cousins whom, up to that point, I had assumed to have been uprooted and unreachable. Sisters Bobbie, Fay, and Cynthia were approximately my age. They were thrilled that we had reconnected, and in no time at all, their wide circle of friends had become mine as well. Their parents, Diana and Solly (son of my father's older brother), opened their home to us, providing food and drink and a warm, convivial spot for socializing.

At length, however, in order to avoid overtaxing their hospitality, we felt obliged to seek a venue where our growing numbers could meet. We landed on northeast London's Leytonstone Maccabean Club, one of several such social centers operated by an Anglo-Jewish society founded in the late 1800s.

Little did I know that such happenstances, such an unfolding succession of everyday events and unremarkable choices, would lead me to the threshold of yet another epochal passage in my life.

# PART TWO
# A NEW ALLEGIANCE

# CHAPTER 4
# AN UNEASY PEACETIME

I had returned to a country whose people and institutions were roiling in political, social, cultural, and economic flux. Nevertheless, we who had survived Nazi Germany's aggressions, soldiers and civilians alike, counted our blessings as we went about the peacetime business of rebuilding interrupted and shattered lives.

At the same time, as good and decent people learned of the atrocities visited upon religious and ethnic minorities by Hitler and his brethren madmen, we wept in anguish and raised our voices to demand justice. The *Holocaust*, as we know, obliterated in excess of six million people of the Jewish faith. Slaughtered, too, were millions of Polish civilians and Soviet prisoners of war, along with significant numbers of Serbs, Gypsies, people with disabilities, and others deemed threatening to the purity of the Aryan 'master race.'

Aside from the sheer magnitude of the number of Jews exterminated, many other factors distinguished their experience from that of other groups. In many parts of Eastern Europe and in the Ukraine, Nazi Germany had willing help in rooting out Jewish populations. Whole family lines disappeared. With rare exceptions, assets of displaced persons, seized and converted, were gone forever. For the most part, those of the Jewish faith struggling to find footing again in the diasporas of Eastern and Western Europe had no home, neither dwelling nor state, which they could call their own.

The following excerpt from the website of the *United States Holocaust Memorial Museum* captures succinctly the essence of the times and those factors which motivated survivors to seek shelter in a Jewish homeland:

During World War II, the Nazis deported between seven and nine million Europeans, mostly to Germany. Within months of Germany's surrender in May 1945, the Allies repatriated to their home countries more than six million displaced persons (DPs; wartime refugees). Between 1.5 million and two million DPs refused repatriation.

Most Jewish survivors, who had survived concentration camps or had been in hiding, were unable or unwilling to return to eastern Europe because of postwar antisemitism and the destruction of their communities during the Holocaust. Many of those who did return feared for their lives. In Poland, for example, locals initiated several violent pogroms. The worst was the one in Kielce in 1946 in which 42 Jews, all survivors of the Holocaust, were killed. These pogroms led to a significant second movement of Jewish refugees from Poland to the west.

At its peak in 1947, the Jewish displaced person population reached approximately 250,000. While the United Nations Relief and Rehabilitation Administration (UNRRA) administered all of the displaced persons camps and centers, Jewish displaced persons achieved a large measure of internal autonomy.

A variety of Jewish agencies were active in the displaced persons camps. The American Jewish Joint Distribution Committee provided refugees with food and clothing, and the Organization for Rehabilitation through Training (ORT) offered vocational training. Jewish displaced persons also formed self-governing organizations, and many worked toward the establishment of a Jewish state in Palestine. There were central committees of Jewish displaced persons in the American and British zones which, as their primary goals, pressed for greater immigration opportunities and the creation of a Jewish homeland in Palestine.

In the United States, immigration restrictions strictly limited the number of refugees permitted to enter the country. The British, who had received a mandate from the League of Nations to administer Palestine, severely restricted Jewish immigration there largely because of Arab objections. Many countries closed their borders to immigration. Despite these obstacles, many Jewish displaced persons attempted to leave Europe as soon as possible.

The Jewish Brigade Group, formed as a unit within the British army in late 1944, worked with "former partisans to help organize the *Brihah* (literally "escape"), the exodus of 250,000 Jewish refugees across closed borders from inside Europe to the coast in an attempt to sail for Palestine. The *Mosad le-Aliyah Bet*, an agency established by the Jewish leadership in Palestine, organized "illegal" immigration (Aliyah Bet) by ship. However, the British intercepted most of the ships.

In 1947, for example, the British stopped the *Exodus 1947* at the port of Haifa. The ship had 4,500 Holocaust survivors on board, who were returned to Germany on British vessels. In most cases, the British detained the refugees – over 50,000 – in detention camps on the island of Cyprus in the eastern Mediterranean Sea. The British use of detention camps as a deterrent failed, and the flood of immigrants attempting entry into Palestine continued.

The internment of Jewish refugees – many of them Holocaust survivors – turned world opinion against British policy in Palestine. The report of the Anglo-American Commission of Inquiry in January 1946 led US president Harry Truman to pressure Britain into admitting 100,000 Jewish refugees into Palestine.

As the crisis escalated, the British government decided to submit the problem of Palestine to the

United Nations (UN). In a special session, the UN General Assembly voted on November 29, 1947, to partition Palestine into two new states, one Jewish and the other Arab, a recommendation that Jewish leaders accepted and the Arabs rejected.

After the British began the withdrawal of their military forces from Palestine in early April 1948, Zionist leaders moved to establish a modern Jewish state. On May 14, 1948, David Ben-Gurion, the chairman of the Jewish Agency for Palestine, announced the formation of the state of Israel, declaring:

> "The Nazi Holocaust, which engulfed millions of Jews in Europe, proved anew the urgency of the reestablishment of the Jewish State, which would solve the problem of Jewish homelessness by opening the gates to all Jews and lifting the Jewish people to equality in the family of nations."

The promise of a promised land – of the establishment of a Jewish state, *Eretz Yisrael* – had roots as old as civilization.

# Chapter 5
# Eretz Yisrael

Yearning for a territorially defined and constitutionally established homeland has been a feature of Jewish culture from ancient times forward. The concept and breadth of *Eretz Yisrael* – the ancestral Land of Israel – have been variously articulated within both the Old Testament and the New Testament. From the very outset, in *Genesis 15:18*, we have:

> The Lord made a covenant with Abram [Abraham], saying, "To your descendants I give this land, from the river of Egypt to the great river, the river Euphrates.[15]

From *Judges 20:1*, the people of Israel dwelled:

> From Dan to Beersheba, including the land of Gilead.[16]

Fulfillment of the covenant would not occur for thousands of years thereafter.

### Diaspora

The Hebrew word for 'exile' is *Galut* (גלות). The *Diaspora* – "dispersion of Jews among the Gentiles"[17] – began with their banishment from Judah by King Nebuchadnezzar II in the 590s to 580s BCE.[18] Exile extended across the ancient world and spread

---

[15] *The Holy Bible*, Thomas Nelson & Sons (New York, 1953).

[16] *Ibid.* Further references in *Exodus*, *Numbers*, *Deuteronomy*, *Samuel*, *Kings*, *Ezekiel*, *Chronicles*, and *Matthew*.

[17] Source: *Encyclopædia Britannica*.

[18] 'Ancient Jewish Diaspora,' *My Jewish Learning*
<https://www.myjewishlearning.com/article/jewish-diaspora/>.

around the globe throughout the centuries and millennia that followed.

The Holy Land, along with huge swaths of southeast and central Europe, western Asia, and North Africa – all were part and parcel of the massive *Ottoman Empire*, an agglomeration of provinces and vassal states ruled by a Turkish monarchy from the early 14th century to the early 20th. Within that span of time, the fortunes of Jewish populations varied widely from positions of influence to objects of persecution. The only certainty for those of the faith was that their status was ever subject to the wicked winds of change for the worse. Then came World War I.

## 'Mandatory Palestine'

Having sided with the Central Powers of Germany and Austria-Hungary against the Triple Entente of Britain, France, and the Russian Empire in waging the 'war to end all wars,' the Ottoman government found itself on the wrong side of history.

Britain, which had asserted provenance in the region through a secret pact made with France during the course of the conflict, succeeded in winning legitimization of its *de facto* hold on Palestine through a *Mandate*, granted by the *League of Nations*, which came into effect on September 29, 1923.

The significance of that act was monumental. Six years before, Arthur James Balfour, U.K. Foreign Secretary, writing to Lord Walter Rothschild, a prominent financier, politician, and leader of the British Jewish Community, openly declared the government's support for establishment of a Jewish homeland. It "represented the beginning of the end of 2,000 years of statelessness," pledging to aid in the effort to create one.[19]

The letter, composed pursuant to a meeting convened five months earlier between Secretary Balfour, Lord Rothschild, and Zionist leader

---

[19] *Balfour Declaration FAQ's*. <u>Source</u>: <u>www.balfour100.com</u>.

Chaim Weizmann[20], became known as the *Balfour Declaration*:

> His Majesty's Government view with favour the
> establishment in Palestine of a national home for the
> Jewish people, and will use their best endeavours to
> facilitate the achievement of this object, it being
> clearly understood that nothing shall be done which
> may prejudice the civil and religious rights of
> existing non-Jewish communities in Palestine, or the
> rights and political status enjoyed by Jews in any
> other country.

The *Balfour Declaration* advanced the cause of Zionism and became a core component of *Mandatory Palestine*. Yet, as would be evidenced by subsequent events, Britain's support for the indigenous population's achievement of the objective proved to be equivocal, varying with the shifting sands of strategic, geopolitical, and economic self-interest.

Another world war would come and go, and once again, the victorious superpowers would divvy up the territorial spoils. Nevertheless, with the exception of the Soviet Union, the Age of Empires was about to bow to its final curtain.

The *League of Nations* effectively passed away on October 24, 1945, the day the *Charter of United Nations* took effect. The newly constituted world body proclaimed its intentions and goals:

> • To practice tolerance and live together in peace
> with one another as good neighbors, and
> • To unite our strength to maintain international

---

[20] *Ibid.* "In 1917 Chaim Weizmann (1874 – 1952) was the indefatigable leader of the Zionist lobby. [He led] the campaign for a British declaration on behalf of Zionism, [having] had his first conversation about [the cause] with Arthur Balfour in January 1906. Years later, Weizmann would become the first President of the State of Israel."

peace and security, and

- To ensure, by the acceptance of principles and the institution of methods, that armed forces shall not be used, save in the common interest, and

- To employ international machinery for the promotion of economic and social advancement of all peoples.

The best of intentions and the rituals of diplomacy were no match, however, for the passions of peoples who had been oppressed, persecuted, and murdered over the course of thousands of years of domination and marginalization. Peoples yearning and struggling to find a decent and safe place in the new world order without having to wait and wait and wait for it to be delivered to them benevolently, if at all.

The Middle East became a boiling cauldron of neighbor against neighbor, allies turned enemies, extremism, and radicalization. Great Britain, caught in a trap of its own making, suffered loss of prestige and precious loss of life in the run-up to the founding of a Jewish homeland.

As noted above in *An Uneasy Peacetime*, on November 29, 1947, the U.N. General Assembly adopted Resolution 181(II), a *Partition Plan for the British Mandate of Palestine*. On May 14, 1948, the *British Mandate* expired. On that day, meeting in Tel Aviv, the *Jewish People's Council* issued a proclamation:

BY VIRTUE OF OUR NATURAL AND HISTORIC RIGHT AND ON THE STRENGTH OF THE RESOLUTION OF THE UNITED NATIONS GENERAL ASSEMBLY, HEREBY DECLARE THE ESTABLISHMENT OF A JEWISH STATE IN ERETZ-ISRAEL, TO BE KNOWN AS THE STATE OF ISRAEL.

Beset by enemies on all sides, Israel would be in for the fight of its life.

# CHAPTER 6
# THE LEYTONSTONE TURNING POINT

The continent was not the sole province of resurgent anti-Semitism after the war. Virulent strains of neo-Nazism had arisen in England, as well. Sir Oswald Mosley, politician and leader of the *British Union of Fascists* from 1932 to 1940, interned by the government at the outbreak of World War II and then granted compassionate release due to illness in 1943, picked up where he had left off after war's end.

In early 1948, he formed the *Union Movement*, an amalgamation of fifty-one separate far-right groups, some of which had staged public meetings in London's East End and other Jewish neighborhoods to instigate confrontations and stoke fear. The movement's banner featured a lightning bolt emulating the shape of the jagged double-*SS* of Nazi Germany's dreaded paramilitary arm, the *Schutzstaffel*.

It was against the backdrop of an open society's tolerance of the very elements of malicious, base nature which had led to the genocidal slaughter of Jews and others that I attended a special event being held at the Leytonstone Maccabean Club one fateful day in mid-May 1948.

Addressing club members and invited guests that evening were two speakers from Palestine – two special emissaries, dispatched by David Ben Gurion, whose express mission was to recruit soldiers for the fight to defend the newly minted State of Israel. I do not remember their names. One was an officer of the *Haganah*, a Jewish paramilitary organization operating within Mandatory Palestine, and the other was of the *Palmach*, an elite forces branch of the *Haganah*.

Arab nations opposed to the UN's two-state design for resolving overlapping Middle East territorial claims had announced their intention to obliterate Israel "before the ink dries on their declaration of independence." Enemy soldiers of the newly formed Arab League[21] were well-trained and well-armed. Many of their commanders were graduates of England's prestigious Sandhurst Military Academy.

All borders of the new state were under threat and on alert. Enemy armies were dug in and poised for the kill. Their orders were to wait for a coordinated signal to attack the infant sovereign state with one massive blow, to *blitzkrieg* à la Hitler, to kill all Jews, to rape their women, to plunder and destroy at large and at will.

The club's spacious all-purpose meeting room was filled to capacity. Within its normally happily chatty confines, you could hear a pin drop.

The *Haganah* commander who spoke first made it clear from the outset that he and his *Palmach* opposite number had come to solicit volunteers. Of course I do not remember what he said word for word, but there is no doubt in my mind that the gist of it went something like this:

> We are in desperate need of experienced men and women to come help defend the new State of Israel. To train our untrained fighting forces. To lead them and teach them how to lead. To serve and fight. We know that many, many here have seen battle. More than enough to last a lifetime. But you have been there in the thick of it. You know how to win. You know what needs to be done and must be done if we are to prevail. For good to vanquish evil. And so we ask, who amongst you is ready and willing to step forward and answer the call?

---

[21] Egypt, Iraq, Lebanon, Saudi Arabia, Syria, and Transjordan.

The commander's words rang in my ears and resonated deeply. I owed my life to the open arms with which Great Britain had accepted my immigrant parents. I was also a Jew, fully cognizant of the sacrifices made by family to preserve heritage and faith. Hitler was dead; Nazi Germany defeated; but lethal anti-Semitism very much alive.

The following notes and observations did not, to the best of my recollection, come to the forefront of my consciousness in that moment to be weighed or deliberated. They were, however, the historical context of my emotional response, dwelling within my head and heart.

## Context of the Head and Heart

Well before Hitler's armed forces attacked Poland in 1939, well before the five-plus years of carnage and ruin that he precipitated, world leaders had squandered clear opportunities to reign in or stymie the megalomaniac's worst impulses.

Not content with having absorbed Austria into imperial Germany in March of 1938, Hitler coveted the *Sudetenland* of neighboring western Czechoslovakia, where approximately three million people of German origin were alleged to reside.

Hitler's warmongering grew increasingly belligerent and threatening, rattling both France, which was contractually allied with Czechoslovakia, and Great Britain. Neither country was prepared to go to war to defend the defenseless.

Negotiations between Britain-and-France and Germany-and-Italy eventually led to the infamous *Munich Agreement*, effectively acceding to Germany's demands. The government of Czechoslovakia had no say in the proceedings. They were forced to accept an internationally sanctioned invasion and occupation.[22]

---

[22] Source: *Encyclopedia Britannica* website <
https://www.britannica.com/event/Munich-Agreement>.

A scant forty days later, world leaders stood by and did nothing beyond official protest when, on the evening of Wednesday, November 9, 1938, Hitler's goons attacked Jews and Jewish properties and institutions throughout Germany. *Kristallnacht*, the 'Night of Broken Glass,' was a harbinger of what was to come: mass murder in the organized, state-run execution of Hitler's *Final Solution*.

Nazi mobs torched or otherwise vandalized hundreds of synagogues throughout Germany and damaged, if not completely destroyed, thousands of Jewish homes, schools, businesses, hospitals and cemeteries. Nearly 100 Jews were murdered during the violence.

Additionally, more than 30,000 Jewish men were arrested and sent to the Dachau, Buchenwald and Sachsenhausen concentration camps, specifically constructed to hold Jews, political prisoners and other perceived enemies of the Nazi state..[23]

**"If not you, then who? If not now, then when?"**

There is an epigram, attributed variously, which warns that The Only Thing Necessary for the Triumph of Evil is That Good People Do Nothing. Two thousand years before I was born, Rabbi Hillel the Elder famously asked, "If not you, then who? If not now, then when?" Did these pithy sayings surface in my thinking at that pivotal moment when David Ben Gurion's spokespersons called for help? No—but the sentiments were there, absolutely.

Was I prepared to leave the creature comforts of a private life, one that I had resumed only relatively recently after a quarter of my young life in uniform? Was I fully cognizant of the implications and potential consequences of joining a foreign force in contravention to my country's laws? Was I truly up to all of it –

---

[23] Source: *The History Channel* website
<www.history.com/topics/holocaust/kristallnacht>.

to forging forward again in harm's way, knowing as I did what fresh hells of death and destruction most assuredly lay ahead?

From a place deep inside came the answers: *yes*, *yes*, and *yes*. They were not words of decision. They were tides of emotion, essences of conscience that carried me forward. Thus did I, an Englishman, a foreigner to Palestine, enlist. Sidney Fersht, *Haganah 76490*, would soon be off to war—again.

# Chapter 7
# SIDNEY FERSHT,
# HAGANAH 76490

Immediately after volunteering, I was instructed to go to a private house in the Stamford Hill area of London, about nine kilometers northeast of center city, where a  man approximately my age asked me a few simple questions: date of birth; military service record; and general state of health. "You'll report to the Jewish Agency in Russell Square," he said flatly after the cursory interview. "They'll send you a telegram with the date and time. 'Chaim awaits you,' it will read. Pack light. Bare necessities only."

It all went according to plan, and swiftly at that. Then came the tough part: having to reveal my act to the family, knowing it would come as a complete surprise and shock to them. Their 'baby brother' leaving to wage war on foreign soil again – an 'elective' war at that—after having served King-and-Country and survived for so long in uniform. But then … it had to be done.

Most difficult to face would be Celia, the eldest of the Fersht clan's first-generation British siblings and, for me particularly, a matriarchal figure and rock of stability. She expressed her disapproval at once. "Why? Why Palestine? Haven't you had enough? You've served your country well and come home healthy and whole. Please, Sidney, why tempt fate?"

Even as she pleaded with me to reconsider, I believe she knew in her heart of hearts that my commitment was irrevocable. Because I had volunteered instinctually, driven by principle, I did not offer an explanation based on a qualitative assessment of pros and cons. There had been no such decision *per se* on my part. There had been only the act of stepping forward to answer the call.

124

In my bones I knew that if I had not done so, and were Israel to be defeated, there would be no way I could live with myself. Thus did I reply as best I could under the emotionally laden circumstances: "Celia dearest, we are not living in this world alone."

Word of my imminent departure spread quickly throughout the rest of the family, many of whom sought to dissuade me from soldiering in Palestine. I empathized with their anxiety. What if it was *my* 'baby brother' or *my* child heading off into the teeth of a shooting war? Nevertheless, it had to be done. Israel needed experienced warriors in order to survive. Who, if not people such as I, would answer the call?

To this day, looking back, I am so proud I maintained the courage of my convictions. Nothing was about to change my mind. I was duty bound to go and serve in whichever ways I could, to help my people – people of a certain faith who had been subjected to murderous repressions for hundreds and thousands of years. One person, I vowed, can make a significant difference.[24]

Brother Judah insisted on driving me to my Russell Square assignation. "That's all you've got?" he asked. "One small suitcase and a raincoat?"

"Travel light. Those were my orders."

"Are you absolutely certain you need to do this?" he pressed. He knew full well what my answer would be, but he felt obliged to give it one final go.

"I am sure, Judah," I replied softly, with gratitude. Bless him for trying.

We motored on in silence. "This is the place," I said as we arrived. "You can wait for me here outside if you like, but I have no idea how long it might take."

"I'll wait," Judah replied. "I'll be right here."

I entered the *Jewish Agency* building and handed my

---

[24] Ultimately, as previously noted, upwards of four thousand *Machalniks* answered the call. Together, we made an enormous difference.

confirmation telegram to the on-duty receptionist. *Chaim awaits you.* He examined it and me in one swift, seamless movement of well-trained eyes. "Follow me, sir," he said, half-inviting and half-ordering. From that point forward, my "induction" proceeded with brisk, businesslike efficiency.

The entire transaction, if you will, took about ten minutes, with no discussion whatsoever. I was handed a slip of paper bearing my name and a note of introduction, written in Hebrew, to the *Jewish Agency* in Paris. "Roll it up; put it away in a pants pocket; and then forget about it until you get there," one of the agency's nameless officials advised.

"These are for you, as well. A one-way ticket from Dover to Calais, then from there to Paris. You are not to converse or associate with anyone. Understood? As soon as you arrive in Paris, you'll go straight to our Paris headquarters on the *Avenue de la Grande Armée*, near to where it begins at *Place de l'Étoile*. Any questions? No? Good."

Hasty handshakes, pats on the back, and expressions of "good luck" and "be safe"—"*shalom, shalom,*" ensued before they ushered me out through the rear entrance.

Former British Naval Intelligence officer Ian Fleming would not write his first *James Bond* novel until four years later,[25] and yet, on that late springtime day in 1948 as I was about to make my way to London Victoria railway station carrying scant belongings and myself into the uncharted territories of intrigue and deception, I felt every bit the covert operative—which, in point of fact, I was. As a British subject, with Great Britain at that time being unallied with the new State of Israel, what I was about to do was illicit – or worse.

I circled around and met up with Judah again. The ride to Victoria was a solemn one. With each of us lost deep in thought, there was a palpable tension – which at last I broke by relating to him the highlights of what had occurred behind the closed doors

---

[25] *Casino Royale*, in 1952.

and curtained windows of the *Jewish Agency*.

When we arrived at the station, Judah didn't want to say goodbye. He parked and walked with me to the platform posted for the first leg of my passage to Palestine. My train was there already, steaming to go. He hardly knew what to do with himself as we neared the designated carriage. Out of the blue, he struck up a conversation with a complete stranger. "This is Sidney," he exclaimed, "my kid brother."

Judah was the kind of person who was always there for you. Always. My dear brother passed away in 2003 at the age of ninety. May he rest in peace.


## Dover

My first, fraught 'undercover' experience occurred at the Port of Dover Customs checkpoint after the contents of my modest valise had been thoroughly searched. Nothing I had packed should have stood out as unusual. From all appearances, I was a simple bloke going on holiday or a casual business trip. And yet, the Customs officer standing opposite me shook his head, stiffened his back, looked me in the eye, and commanded, "Follow me, Sir."

"What?" What had I done? What did he find that made him want to question me? Was it my RAF sweater? Could that be it? Did that constitute a tell?

"Right this way, then." His tone was steeped in officialdom. I was in trouble. He led me to a small, windowless room at the rear of the main Customs hall. "Empty your pockets, Sir."

I made a show of fussing about in my right front pants pocket as I jangled a bunch of coins while kneading my Hebrew language letter of introduction into a nondescript wad. He proceeded to pat me down from head to foot. My heart began to race. Nipped in the bud. Detained and possibly arrested at the demarcation point between two flags. Some secret agent I was!

"Where are you off to, soldier?" he asked as he continued to probe my clothing, crotch, and armpits for contraband or concealed weapons. "How long do you plan to be out of country?"

"Switzerland!" I blurted out. "Hiking." Why that particular lie came tumbling out over my lips, I haven't the foggiest. "I'll be there as long as the money lasts." Outwardly, my demeanor suggested I was telling the truth. Inside, I mocked myself for coming up with such an outlandish explanation. There were no hiking boots in my kit and no other equipment remotely suitable for mountaineering. Only that gosh awful giveaway RAF sweater.

"Switzerland. Hiking. Right you are," he sniped. "And I'm a direct descendant of Saint Brigid of Kildare. I know exactly where you're off to: *Palestine*."

My expression revealed nothing. I channeled my apprehension into annoyance. "You've haven't searched *this* pocket yet," I ventured sarcastically, rattling pence and tuppence as I extracted my hand. What brass balls I had to invite inspection as a ploy to deter it. Or lunacy.

"Save it. You'll need more than good luck where you're headed. Those Arabs – you can't trust a single one of them. Smile in your face while they're knifing you in the back first chance they get if you're not careful."

"Thank you for looking out for my welfare."

He did not appreciate thinly veiled sarcasm. "We're done here. So off with you, then. But know this: we *will* get you on your return. Have no doubt."

The Customs' officer's concern for a Jew's safety in the hostile sands of the Middle East, whether real or feigned, caused me to chuckle inside. Irony was rampant. Fresh in my memory were the admonitions given those of us in uniform in India to watch our backs and travel only in pairs. Militants within Mahatma Gandhi's *Quit India Movement* were known to wield cudgels, knives, garrotes, and other murderous devices in pressing their cause. And here was this unmistakably Irish inquisitor, in British Customs officers' uniform no less, taking me to task for answering a new nation's rallying cry for independence, when all the while parts of his own birth country were striving to throw off the yoke of British rule.

The Customs hall, a cavernous converted airplane hangar, had cleared. The only object of investigation remaining in sight was my splayed-open valise with its contents lumped in a heap. From a distance, people were shouting to me. "Hurry up! You're holding up the ferry!" I hustled to cram my clothing back into the case. It wouldn't close. I broke out into a sweat and improvised, using my raincoat belt as a strap to bundle it up. What I couldn't fit in, I tucked under one arm as I hastened out the door. I heard peals of laughter from passengers at the rail as I scurried up the boarding ramp. I must have looked like a bumbling fool to them.

I felt humiliated. *I've just been treated like a criminal*, I wanted to shout back. *By the very same country under whose flag I served and fought and nearly died defending. Yes, I'm a Jew. On my way to Palestine. That is no laughing matter.*

## Channel Crossing

Once on deck, I sought out a quiet, private place where I could sort out my jumbled belongings and unsettled thoughts. I couldn't get that intimidating Customs officer out of my head. He as much as implied that my leaving to fight for Israel constituted a traitorous act. Sadly, in the eyes of my birth country, he wasn't far off the mark. The British government had branded as terrorists elements of Palestine's indigenous Jewish militias. Neither forgotten nor forgiven was the murder of British citizens by the *Irgun* in the King David Hotel bombing two years before.

I found an interior corner spot, away from heavy foot traffic, where I managed handily to reassemble my gear. Now I would look respectable to those who had judged me a bumpkin. Getting my head straight – that was a different matter. *You're a British subject, Sidney. What are your priorities? Does that word even apply? How can you rank allegiances* plural? *Or is there an allegiance surpassing borders, an allegiance to an immutable, overarching principle?*

The process of self-examination itself helped, even if the

questions remained only partially and inconsistently answered. My conscience remained clear. I affirmed my resolve, wedded to my non-decision decision.

The choppy channel crossing matched my mood. Thoughts of the *Stirling Castle*, which had carried me from England's southern shores for the first time years before, sprang to mind. Some of her cargo of fresh-faced warriors had failed to return. They were with me now in spirit.

By the time the ferry docked at Calais, I was beginning to feel like my old self again. Feisty. Searching. Self-reliant. Motivated by a spirit of adventure. I had dismissed mental images of armed adversaries massed on the borders of Israel, lurking, prowling, ready to pounce. Back in the day, when the Jerry's wolfpack U-boats had menaced the very same waters now plied by the ferry carrying me to Calais, I'd done the same. Rejecting feelings of dread is bound up in the survival instinct.

## Paris

From Calais it was on to Paris via Lille by train, a rail distance of roughly 340 kilometers or 211 miles, traveling third class on a coach car of the *Chemins de Fer du Nord*. Hours after departure, the iron horse chugged and wheezed into the splendid Beaux-Art terminal *Gare du Nord*, built more than one hundred years before with massive steel pillars smelted in Glasgow.

Walking the streets of the City of Lights for the first time in my life was a treat. So many of its fabled venues, structures, and coursing avenues had been etched into the mind's eye through photographs and cinema newsreels. A shiver of excitement ran through me as I turned a corner and caught sight of the full extent of the Eiffel Tower, from its splayed four-footed base to the nubby peak of its giraffe-like outstretched neck.

Along the way, I had passed by specialty shops and restaurants scenting the sidewalk air with tantalizing aromas of yeasty baked breads and savory roasted meats. *Boulangerie. Pâtisserie. Brasserie. Bistro.* My stomach realized before I did that I hadn't eaten a bite since leaving home that morning. I was famished. At the very next opportunity, I popped into a café which, from the outside, appeared to be decent *and* inexpensive.

I did a good job, I thought, navigating the all-in-French menu, of which I understood not one word – other than *bifteck*. That, I deduced, had to be beefsteak. And indeed it was yummy, if a bit gamey. I relished every morsel of the charbroiled slab, washing it down with an entire large carafe of red table wine. Pleasantly sated, I patted my tummy and stood to pay *l'addition* and leave. The room started to revolve around me. Ah, Paris!

Days later, when I related the story of my inaugural Parisian day to newly made friends, they delighted in providing me with a French language lesson. "*Bifteck* doesn't mean *beefsteak*, Sidney. *Bifteck* is steak. Any kind of steak. *Bifteck de Cheval*, which is what *you* had, is a specialty cut – steak meat carved from a *cheval*. From a horse, Sidney. *Bon appétit!*"

## The Jewish Agency, Paris

Entering the *Jewish Agency* building in Paris, I experienced sensations identical to those that had gripped me when I'd stepped into its counterpart in London: electric excitement and mounting anticipation. World War II Veteran and Covert Operative Sidney Fersht, *Haganah 76490*, reporting for duty, ready to receive orders for the next leg of a clandestine passage to Palestine.

With chagrin, I produced and handed over a crumpled, tattered letter of introduction, which I had squeezed down surreptitiously to the size of a misshapen marble whilst the Dover Customs martinet put me through my paces. I explained in detail to the desk clerk what had happened. He nodded knowingly. "You're far from the first who's been searched and interrogated by that particular meddlesome fellow," he acknowledged. "We'll see what we can do about him."

What could they *possibly* do about him? Unless, by some slim chance, they had managed to plant a mole inside British Customs services. I might have been 'far from the first,' but it was I who was on the spot that one ferry ride ago, and I considered myself fortunate that Mr. Irishman hadn't arranged to have a pistol planted in my luggage as a pretext for arresting me. The Customs hall had been vacated by the time he'd finished grilling and searching me. There would have been ample opportunity for one of his cohorts to set me up and make an example of me. I'd be looking at serious jailtime. Imagine the headlines:

## Armed Terrorist Arrested

Dover Customs Officer Nabs Ex-R.A.F.

Sidney Fersht Bound for Palestine

I shuddered to think about it.


## Next Leg

Those who had been directed to the *Jewish Agency*'s Parisian portal came from a cross-section of backgrounds, nationalities, and ethnicities, including native North African Jews. At one point, the thought crossed my mind that our French Zionist movement hosts had managed to locate and assemble representatives from each of the biblical twelve Hebrew tribes.

There was no time to waste. From Paris, we were transported by truck some 780 kilometers south-southeast to a campsite situated in the outskirts of Trets, a medieval commune in the mountainous Provence-Alpes-Côtes d'Azur region, roughly one-hour's drive northeast of the port city of Marseille.

Throughout the duration of our brief stay at the transit camp, we were obliged to remain within its confines. There, I soon made the acquaintance of other volunteers such as Mark Compton, an elite forces infantryman veteran hailing from the Midlands, and Eddie Weisfish, a Dutchman – both of whom became good friends as we traveled and trained together.

The majority of our number, however, had not borne arms in uniform. They were displaced refugees and survivors who had managed to cheat Hitler's *Final Solution* by dint of their own courage and cunning, and with the invaluable help of resistance fighters and selfless humanitarians who had risked all to save them.

Trets and its environs were chosen for our preliminary 'induction' and training as its elevation and terrain were deemed by our handlers to be akin to conditions we might expect to encounter in the hills of Galilee, a likely ultimate destination we were told.

We were bivouacked within a rustic chalet-like building, close by a classic French countryside chateau. Some of the lodge's floorboards had been removed for the purpose of concealing arms and ordnance, including reconditioned *Bren* light machineguns and a clutch of grenades.

Firing pins had been removed from pistols, rifles, and automatic weapons, as they were for instructional purposes only. For those of us who had been instrumental in bringing about the destruction of the Third Reich and earning the celebration of V-E Day, such play-acting with mute weaponry was a ridiculous waste of time.

I remember distinctly our two instructors, Uri and Baruch, both admirable, ranking *Haganah* Israelis. Daytimes, they led us in mountaineering – climbing, climbing, ever climbing – sometimes skirting the edge of ultra-narrow footpaths alongside which sheer, nearly vertical escarpments portended certain death for the incautious hiker. I don't mind confessing that those moments scared the heck out of me. If I dared look down, I'd break out into a blooming sweat.

Uri and Baruch taught us how to scale rock ridges reaching twelve to fifteen feet high, using only hands and feet for the ascension. We'd straddle the peak, turn to face the other side, elongate our bodies by hanging onto the ridgeline with both hands, then bend knees and drop to a safe landing with our legs serving as shock absorbers.

Though our location and mission were supposed to be closely guarded secrets, the activities associated with the transit camp were bound to attract attention. One morning, one of my fellow *Machalniks*-in-training came running over, warning that a British reporter was moseying around the camp, asking lots of questions as he sought to identify and speak with British citizen-soldiers.

I was advised to stay out of sight for a while. For all we knew, the man could have been a snoop from Her Majesty's Secret Intelligence Service, MI6. Later on, I learned that he was a stringer for London's *Daily Mirror*, nosing about for a story. Either way, it was best to lie low, lest evidence confirming Israel's organized campaign to enlist the aid of people such as me, British subject-veterans, become a diplomatic flashpoint between England and France.

We of the Jewish faith owe a debt of gratitude to the French government and people of that time. National, regional, and local authorities looked aside discreetly, tacitly granting Jewish refugees and others dedicated to the cause unchallenged passage through their country to the docklands of Marseille. Once safely there, the volunteers embarked on all manner of watercraft bound for the shores of the Holy Land.

Of course, the whole world knew exactly what France was doing, in effect supporting the mission of *Aliyah Bet*,[26] immigration to Mandatory Palestine in defiance of British law. But who would venture first to make an issue of it, when the whole world knew full well that positions on the matter had been driven

---

[26] "Between the end of World War II in 1945 and the beginning of the Israeli-Arab war of 1948-49, Palestinian Jews had two great needs. One was humanitarian, the other was military. Their first need was to rescue several hundred thousand Holocaust survivors trapped in displaced persons camps throughout Europe. At the time, there was a British naval blockade preventing all but a handful (the quota was 1,250 Jewish immigrants per month) from coming to the British-controlled Palestine mandate. Ships had to be quietly purchased, then crews had to be found who were willing to man the ships and risk British imprisonment to smuggle the 'illegal' immigrants into Palestine. This rescue operation was called Aliyah Bet ('Immigration B,' the term used for clandestine immigration)." Source: *The Story of Aliyah Bet and Machal*, Aliyah Bet & Machal Virtual Museum <http://www.israelvets.com/>.

by the United Kingdom's addiction to oil from the oil-rich sands of the Arab Middle East? Politicians in power had sacrificed fundamental decency and regard for human life for the assurance of an uninterrupted supply of black gold energy.

Arab leaders, manifestly aware of the strategic advantage such fortuitous possession of coveted natural resources provided them, leveraged their control of the tap. *You want oil, Great Britain? You want oil, United States of America? Play along.*

Soon after our instructors had satisfied themselves that our motley crew had made the most of their rudimentary training exercises, they ordered us to pack up and prepare for travel – from Trets to Marseille – and from there via ship to Tel Aviv.

Uri and Baruch met with about thirty of us beforehand. "You've been selected to serve as security on the ship. As deputies, to help police good order. The *Monte Chiaro* flies the flag of Italy, but we own it.[27] Up until now, we've used it to smuggle arms. This time, people."

We could only surmise that they chose us from amongst the eight hundred or so men and women who would be onboard based upon our military service records – information that they had assembled as we advanced through the pipeline.

After having been trucked to coastal Marseille and deposited dockside, we trekked across a makeshift causeway consisting of a string of pontoon floats toward a ship appearing to be no larger than a modest-size cross-river ferryboat. Two municipal *gendarmes*, swaying and humming under the influence of too

---

[27] "During Dec. 1947 to Mar. 1948, the [David Ben Gurion's] 'acquisition' organizers purchased six ships for transporting the arms – Santa-Chiara, Ressurectio, Maestralle, Monte-chiaro, Scio and Nora. For obvious reasons, the ships continued to carry foreign flags and were operated by their foreign crews. For 'safety reasons.' the *Mossad* placed on board every ship an escort – *Palyam* naval cadets and *Gideonees* (the nom the guerre for *Haganah* radio operators)." – Yehuda Ben-tzur, *A Matter of Survival: The Early Stages of the Arms Procurement Enterprise*, published online, Palyam & Aliyah Bet Website <http://www.palyam.org/indexEn>.

much *vin de pays* or *absinthe*, stood guard as we made our way. Having been well taken care of beforehand with fistfuls of paper currency, they offered no resistance to our exodus.

The *Monte Chiaro*, the '*Bright Mountain*,' belying her christened name, was anything but. On boarding her, my first impression was a most pessimistically unflattering one: *My God, we're all going to sink and die.* Clearly, the bucket, having seen better days, was ever so much more well-suited for drydock and the scrapheap than for an uncertain journey across the open, heavily patrolled waters of the Mediterranean Sea.

My chum Mark Compton, also deputized to the security detail, clued me in as to the pedigree of the *Monte Chiaro*. She was a resurrection, sunk during wartime off the coast of Canada, then dredged up from the depths and minimally refitted, with Zionist funding, for service.

Once bearing arms shipments bound for Mandatory Palestine, she would now be shuttling refugees, émigrés – and *Machalniks* – to the Holy Land.

Eight hundred souls spent nine stuffy, stinking days in ultra-cramped quarters, converted cargo holds belowdecks, subsisting on meager rations. Though most everyone had endured years of extreme privation and had escaped the jaws of death and gates of hell to get there, conditions on the *Monte Chiaro*, degrading and at times horrific, taxed nerves and patience to the Nth degree. Making port at Tel Aviv on July 19, 1948, came none too soon.

Once again, I stood at the high perch rail of a ship, taking in the sights and sounds of a thriving port. Soon I would be stepping foot on a patch of land that had been conquered time and again by outside powers bending it to their will. *Our* foreign invasion, however, was a friendly one, by the sons and daughters of the Diaspora. Mandatory Palestine was no more. The Jewish people had struggled, bled, and died to claim their God-given right, their Promised Land, now proudly flying the flag of the two-month-old State of Israel.

I recall taking a long, reflective moment, absorbing all that was happening about me. A gut feeling welled up, which even now is difficult to describe in the fullness of its impact on my being. I *belonged*. I was proud to be a Jew, to be able through service to honor and reward the courage of my forebears. This was *their* Israel, too. Not only would I be witnessing history in the making, but God willing I would be helping to make it happen, too.

As if on cue, the sounds of violins and choral voices came wafting magically over the waters, transporting our spirits with the playing of *Hatikvah* ('The Hope'), the longtime Zionist anthem that would become that of Israel.

*Hello, Israel. My name is Sidney Fersht. Haganah 76490. I am a Machalnik.*

Technically, however, I was also a man without a country. On shipboard, the leading *Haganah* commander, medium-built, but fighting fit and tough as nails, had collected my passport. "For safekeeping," he said. "In case we're intercepted and boarded by a British patrol boat. They'd haul you off in a heartbeat."

Doubtless, he did much the same with all of us, amassing passports 'just in case.' When we put in at Tel Aviv, there was no mention of returning them to their former possessors. One way or another, each of us had become a *de facto* immigrant.

Two of our passenger refugees were expectant mothers in their third trimester. They had been provided with sleeping accommodations apart from the main body cramped belowdecks and had managed to remain healthily pregnant throughout the long, ocean-buffeted voyage. Their babies would be born *Sabra*, native Israeli Jews who, would go on to have children of their own, with generations to follow.[28]

---

[28] In recollecting these thoughts today, it gives me pleasure to believe that the grandchildren and great-grandchildren of those two determined women are fully cognizant of the fact that the roots of their existence were delivered to Israel and planted onshore by the *Monte Chiaro*, a converted cargo ship belonging to founding father David Ben Gurion's ragtag fleet of life-saving, life-affirming vessels.

As the *Monte Carlo* began disgorging its human cargo onto the docks, it was manifestly evident what each of the disembarking passengers was thinking and feeling. Their first reaction on planting their feet was to kneel down and kiss the newly hallowed ground. The looks on their radiant faces spoke volumes. Eretz Yisrael. *Their* Eretz Yisrael.

Their safe arrival was nothing short of a miracle. Having been prey for so long to Hitler's relentless genocidal madness, many had become dehumanized, wretchedly animalistic, unable to relate to others. They never dreamt they would be capable again of experiencing the profound gift of deliverance. Yet here they were, hearts warming, tears of joy streaming freely, smiling, laughing, hugging, experiencing a rebirth of dignity and hope.

I joined them in exultation. And yet, soon thereafter, my elation yielded to a pressing matter of self-interest. My one fervent wish, to the exclusion of all others, was to find a place as soon as possible where I could shower or bathe. It had been ten days since cleansing water touched my crud-crusted skin, and I stunk to high heaven – so much so that I couldn't stand to be near me.

The sights and sounds of dockside hustle and bustle were reassuringly familiar. Newly recruited traffic wardens dressed in British-style khaki uniforms did their best to tame the vehicular chaos, emulating their one-time British overlords with arm and wrist movements typically seen in the roundabouts of Piccadilly and Oxford Circus.

Gathered at the shoreline to greet those disembarking were families and friends of many. Complete strangers stood by to welcome them, too, grateful as they were to witness yet another boatload of volunteers flowing in to join the cause.

We, the *Monte Chiaro* contingent, were directed to move ourselves and our minimal belongings toward waiting vehicles. Commands, shouted in Hebrew, meant nothing without the hand gestures which accompanied them. My childhood Torah and Haftarah *bar mitzvah* lessons didn't help one iota. Sign language, though, *that* I understood.

The ride from the port to our provisional quarters at *Tel Litvinsky*, a nearby British military encampment until termination of the Mandate, was a thankfully short one. We were filthy, famished, and exhausted, and by-and-large we addressed those needs in that order.

I showered long and greedily, ate like a horse (after all, I'd eaten one in Paris), and hit the sack in a communal dormitory where, hope against hope, I'd rest undisturbed forever and a day, replenishing fatigued muscles and sleep-starved organs.

Or so I thought.

# CHAPTER 8
# THE HOLY LAND

Our rude awakening came suddenly, in the middle of the night. The man raising the alarm appeared to be borderline berserk as he ran pall mall through the dormitory, banging on doors, bellowing "Get out! Get out! Get out!" at the top of his lungs in one language after another.

My heart and mind were racing. *We must be under attack. Either that or the building's on fire.*

I snatched my shoes and whatever articles of clothing were within easy reach, then fled the premises along with everyone else. Outside, there was neither smoke nor fire. Nor were we receiving incoming rounds.

Instead, at first reckoning, it appeared that our reception committee had decided to subject us 'raw recruits' to a snap drill. As each of us exited, we were issued a vintage British Lee-Enfield bolt-action rifle and an upside-down banged-up helmet cradling loose rounds of ammo. Some of our lot hadn't had time to zip up their pants as fighting gear was thrust into their hands. "Hurry up, there, onto the trucks!"

Our transport vehicles had been growling the entire time, adding to the sense of chaotic urgency. With a gnash of gears and spitting of gravel from the drivetrain tires, we were off.

"What's happening? Where are we going?" called a voice from the rear, at high pitch to be heard over the din of engine noise and multiple languages competing for air space simultaneously.

"To a kibbutz on the frontier," replied the driver, with oddly calm detachment. "They're under attack. They need help. Reinforcements. We're the reinforcements."

As the initial wave of panic waned and the contingent began to settle down, I conducted my own inventory of thoughts and emotions. *What am I doing here, squatting down in the rear of a ramshackle truck, my hands wrapped around an artifact of weaponry, when we very well could be delivered smack dab into a hot zone, encountering trained enemy soldiers with modern gear?* Such apprehension was exacerbated by the behavior of the people around me, carrying on like carefree schoolchildren going on some kind of treasure hunt. They were actually pointing their rifles at one another, laughing as they pretended to shoot. A trained soldier would never do that; there is always the chance the rifle is loaded with one in the chamber.

The man had claimed we were being sent as reinforcements. The very idea was ludicrous at best, when it was plain to see that no more than a handful of our lot had ever held, much less fired, a ballistic weapon. *God help us.*

Sitting next to me were the Rosenberg brothers, identical twins whom I had first met at Trets. They spoke very little English. "Have you ever fired one of these?" I asked, miming the act for emphasis. They shook their heads. *No.*

What came next was so bizarre, that had we not been heading for all we knew into pitched battle, it might have been uproariously funny.

I decided right then and there to instruct the Rosenberg twins on the safe and proper ways to load, ready, aim, and fire their rifles. To load, I demonstrated, one must first remove the safety catch and then, aiming the working end of the barrel upwards, far away from line-of-sight with people, slide a jacketed bullet into the chamber.

As I slid the bolt back into firing position, the bullet jammed tight in the chamber. *What the bloody hell?* A close inspection revealed the culprit: an incompatible round. The thoroughly British Lee-Enfield takes a thoroughly British .303 inch caliber shell. Somehow, an errant bullet had made its way into my helmet. Only a shell with the same diameter, length, and tapering profile of the .303 would do – in other words, only ammo made specifically for the Lee-Enfield. How many other such bogies might have been tossed haphazardly into the mix? A shiver ran through me. All it would take is one such impostor to cause a weapon to seize up and become inoperative, thereby dooming its bearer in the midst of a firefight.

*My first full day in Israel, and we're heading into combat ill-armed and untrained. A royal cock-up and exercise in futility What have I gotten myself into?*

So as not to reignite passions and panic, I determined to keep that grim information to myself for the time being. My prudence was soon rewarded. The kibbutz, as it turned out, was *not* under attack. Whether it was bad information or garbled communications, the dust-up had been a false alarm. The outcome, had we actually been thrust into a field thick with flying bullets and mortar fire, would have been disastrous. The Arabs would have had a turkey shoot.

For peace of mind and good measure, we stood watch at the kibbutz for several hours. The residents put out salads and refreshments, thanked us for our service, and waved goodbye as we returned to our transports. By midday, we were back in *Tel Litvinsky*. Our lesson in futility had concluded with no loss of life. Thank the Lord! How lucky can one be?


## The Swearing-In Parade

Fresh off the trucks, we were directed to form an assembly by a diminutive, heavyset Israeli soldier who demonstrably considered it essential to assert his authority by announcing his rank (corporal) and standing as commander of the moment. He issued his orders rapidly, in a succession of languages, of which broken, barely decipherable English was one.

"What's he want us to do?" called someone close by. "He wants us to fall in," I replied. "Columns of three. Apparently, we're going to be pledging allegiance to the new State of Israel."

The event would have been humorously entertaining, instead

of pathetic, had the country not been at war. The phrase *columns-of-three* did not translate well. Bedlam reigned as the play-acting soldiers, conversing excitedly in a Babel of languages, scurried about in random patterns, coalescing in knots and then peeling off to find some other, presumably superior place to be.

Mark Compton and I, being savvy about such things, marched smartly to the front of the parade ground and stood at attention, a quite natural, automatic movement for veterans such as we. Mark's frame, ramrod straight, formed a perfect ninety degree angle to the earth beneath him, as if he were awaiting review by his elite forces commandant of yore.

Unwittingly, we had become the straight-men in the scene. When the scurrying about had finally come to an end – after sustained, ineffectual shouting and gesturing by Corporal Columns-of-Three – the curled, crisscrossed lines resembled a hopelessly tangled knot of human corkscrews.

With the six-pointed *Magen David* (the *Star of David*) standard hoisted on a pole and undulating in the breeze, we took our oath of fealty to the newly anointed Promised Land of Israel. Once again, my heart swelled with pride.

The doughty corporal made one final, fruitless attempt at drill practice soldiering, issuing multilingual orders to dismiss, turn right, turn left, and so on. Another spectacular circus ensued.

Mark and I looked at one another as if to say, "Holy hell! What have we gotten ourselves into?" War is serious business. As serious as it gets. If this first day in Israel – running around like a freshly decapitated chicken from the wee hours of the morning – was any indication of what was to follow, then we were in for a world of hurt.

Mark determined right then and there to act to avert the worst. He elected to leave the main body of the *Haganah* and apply, instead, for a frontline position in its special forces *Palmach* division, where he became a gunner in the one of its highly mobile mechanized units.

*A wise move, my friend.*

## Another Field Commission

In short order, things happened very quickly. Without prior notice or so much as a brief reinterview affirming my background and experience, I was promoted to take complete charge of the camp's new arrivals.

My orders were the epitome of unadorned economy of words: "Make soldiers out of them." The men running *Tel Litvinsky* knew that the incoming pools of refugees needed to receive military training and team-building exercises. They didn't wait for permission. There was no time to waste in bureaucracy and red tape. Improvisation, adaptation, and self-reliance were the orders of the day, every day. They were fighting for their lives.

When I was informed of my appointment, the sheer weight of the onus of responsibility so overwhelmed me that my brain simply shut down for a few moments. I was in shock. The full import didn't register. For quite some time thereafter, the words *make soldiers out of them* echoed again and again in my mind.

What I do recall, with crystal clarity, is that when my command position was announced in camp, I was instantly surrounded by hundreds of those refugees with whom I had sailed on the *Monte Chiaro*. The moment is etched in memory as, concurrently, there came a tap on my shoulder by an American fellow who introduced himself as Captain Norman Schutzman. "You're taking over my command," he said. "Good luck."

Just like me, impelled by conscience, Schutzman had volunteered to fight for the new state when he learned of the peril threatening its existence. Sixty-seven years after having served as a *Machalnik*, Norman Schutzman described the moment in his autobiography:

> The more I kept thinking about re-establishing the State of Israel after 2,000 years of homelessness as well as the Holocaust and the death of 6 million Jewish people, I knew that I would have to do everything possible to help. As the news became worse and 15th May drew closer, I realized that as a committed Jew,

what I had to do was to volunteer and join the Haganah. When I told my parents of this decision, they were aghast. We had great arguments. They couldn't understand how anyone who had been in the US army for four years, had served in the Pacific and Europe and still came out alive, would now willingly tempt fate and put his life on the line. I remember vividly telling them that if I didn't go, I would never be able to live with myself.[29]

Eight years prior to that transfer of command, I too, like the hundreds now depending on me, had been a nestling in the nest. To acquit myself well and to honor their courage with effective leadership and training, I would need to draw on all of the learning, experience, and expertise that I had received and acquired throughout that span. And that I did.

I drew on the order, instructional methods, and rigor of my six-weeks-long boot camp. I drew on my gunnery training, my clerking in a squadron office orderly room, and the many other posts and positions of responsibility that had come my way – anything and everything from which pertinent and effective systems and tools could be distilled. Even the legacy spirit of my resourcefulness as a fourteen-year-old lad thrust into the labor force, having to make the best of the worst of circumstances, came into play.

To pull it all off, I would need the assistance and support of a cadre of similarly experienced volunteers – men *and* women, of whom there were several. Most fortunately, many answered the call, becoming both essential support staff and my inspiration for the mission at hand.

With the aid of an Israeli interpreter, we began by building a roster of all the newly sworn-in soldiers, one at a time. It was a laborious process, but one that would pay dividends. We made

---

[29] Source: 'Norman Schutzman' excerpt published online by *World Machal* <http://www.machal.org.il/>, citing *My Personal Relationship with Israel*, N. Norman Schutzman (self-published, USA, 2015).

note of each person's name, *Haganah* service number, nationality, native language, second languages, if any, and date of birth. With that information in hand, we were able to establish appropriately constituted platoons of about thirty to thirty-five, numbering and sorting the units so that we could then structure an effective and efficient chain-of-command.

Each platoon featured a designated instructor and, if necessary, a translator who also served as second-in-command. Befitting our bootstrap operation, individual instructors had full authority to manage their platoons as they saw fit. Some chose to promote certain men in the ranks to the equivalent of lance corporal, distinguishing their service and thereby motivating others.

Setting up a base camp to train our platoons was not an issue, as we had inherited the compound recently vacated by departing British military personnel. With the lowering of the *Union Jack* and the raising of the *Magen David*, Mandatory Palestine had passed into the pages of history two months before, some twenty-eight years after it had been imposed on the region by the League of Nations.

What I would have given to be there that day in the capital, to have been present at the creation, as the flag waved and the *Hatikvah* was sung for the very first time on the home soil and in the heady air of statehood.

In addition to barracks, latrines, cookhouse, mess hall, brig, armory, warehouse, and medical facility, the camp boasted the fundamentals needed for basic training: firing ranges and obstacle courses. Yes, the equipment was old to elderly, but serviceable if maintained and arguably good enough for instructional purposes. Uniforms, however, were simply not available and would not be forthcoming. Having them would have given us a leg up on building an *esprit de corps*.

Yet, even though we in command lacked insignia, bars, or other visible signs of rank, our recruits came to appreciate and respect us for who we were and what we brought to the table. To the unknowing eye, we may have looked like an odd, loosely knit

146

band of guerilla fighters. Odd? Perhaps. Loosely knit? Not after we'd done our bit. Guerilla fighters? I should certainly hope so.

In fact, it wasn't very long before we and our men knew with confidence that they had acquired the skills, stamina, discipline, and team spirit to serve well and proudly in allegiance to the new State of Israel. Rigorous routines in weapons training, physical exercise, combat skills and tactics, chain-of-command protocols – all of these, practiced again and again and again, turned that jumble of corkscrews into a proud fighting force.

I must add, however, that our aptitudes and dedication to task as instructors were not solely responsible for accomplishing the transformation. The metamorphosis had been fostered from within the men as well. I could sense that their attitudes toward life itself had undergone a sea change from dismal to bright.

After untold years of unimaginable suffering, they were finding a purpose in life at last. Training made them stronger and more confident, turning the venom that had built and been bottled up inside them into aspiration, motivation, and passion. So, so many of them had experienced tragic, unspeakable loss firsthand.

For them, the magnetic attraction of the opportunity for retribution and redemption was fierce and irresistible. I had no doubt that they were capable of great courage and would be fearless warriors, even and especially in situations where the enemy might appear to have the advantage of numbers.

The words that delivered me to that remarkable turning point echoed yet again in my mind – this time as an anthem in and of itself: *Make Soldiers Out of Them.* Together, we had.

# CHAPTER 9
# PASSAGES

When off duty, I would travel into center city Tel Aviv and visit Maxim's, a bar-and-eatery on Hayarkon Street, where *Machalniks* would gather to hang out, exchange stories, and recharge their batteries. I looked forward to connecting with good friend Mark Compton; with David Susman, a South African whose experience in volunteering had, like that of Captain Schutzman, paralleled my own;[30] with Jeff Perlman, Susman's fellow South African; and with many others, including an American from Chicago who went by the nickname 'Eskimo.'

With such communality of purpose and camaraderie-in-arms, one would expect Maxim's to be a melting pot of cultures and customs, that language barriers and engrained habits would not impede sociability. But they did, nonetheless. The fact that most all of us were Jews did not alter the equation. Generations and centuries in which diverse ethnic groups had lived in relative isolation within the *Diaspora* made it difficult for us to relate to one another. Jews from Western Europe, Eastern Europe, the Middle East, South Africa, America, Great Britain, the Soviet Union – we were not the same, irrespective of shared faith.

---

[30] "Father was horrified. Just when it appeared that I would settle into a responsible life, with a degree tucked under my belt, I would be putting this, and, said he, my very life, at risk again. How could I be so irresponsible? To his added irritation, I took the high ground. How could a Jew stand by when the very existence of the remnants of our people was threatened after the nightmare of the Holocaust? If the Arabs succeeded in destroying the new State of Israel, no young Jew could live with the memory that he, personally, might have helped save the situation." <u>Source</u>: 'David Susman' excerpt published online by *World Machal* <http://www.machal.org.il/>, citing Susman's memoir, *An African Shopkeeper*.

Despite our being united in common cause, it was the little things which drove some of us nuts – such as relentless cadging for cigarettes or 'spare change' by the down-and-outers. Or eating habits. Or other vexing behaviors and eccentricities. Eventually some of our friends tried to get us situated in a privately organized club for English-speaking soldiers only. But no, that would not do. Segregation was anathema, and it cut both ways. We rejected the idea forthwith.

The saga of Israel's bloody, albeit relatively brief, *War of Independence* is well-documented. The conflict was marked by two third-party-mediated armistice truce agreements, both of which failed to hold. The first, widely violated on both sides, commenced June 11, 1948, and ceased twenty-eight days later. The second such nominal pause, from July 18 through October 15, fared no better. Hostilities continued, with Israeli forces continuing in the main to best their opponents in winning battles and gaining territory. A third truce began that same day, October 15, and yet the battles raged on. Only in early 1949 did most of the parties to the regional war consent to sign and abide by separate bilateral armistice agreements with Israel: Egypt on February 24; Lebanon on March 23; Jordan on April 3; and Syria on July 20. Iraq's withdrawal from the fields of battle was covered by Israel's pact with Jordan.

The brokered peace, if one can call it that, enabled the young country to catch its collective breath, safeguard its gains, rebuild, and build anew. Infantry troops from *Tel Litvinksky*'s highly improvisational training school had earned their piece of history in the effort. By helping to right the wrongs of the past, they had helped to secure the promise of a just and righteous future.

In the run-up to cessation of hostilities, knowing that my mission and that of my command staff had been met, I began to look for fresh challenges and opportunities. I managed to secure a new posting, linking up with an Israeli Air Force unit stationed in the Negev, due south of Tel Aviv.

I expected there to be more action, but operations appeared to be winding down. All I can remember doing was filling oil lamps lining the perimeter of a dusty airstrip in order to facilitate nighttime sorties. The fighting had not ceased entirely. People were still being killed and wounded. Thus, for howsoever long as there were jobs to be done in support of the cause, I would do them. I would continue to do my bit.

Again the local kibbutz tended to our daily needs – 'room and board.' Most of our meals consisted of Middle Eastern style cold salads with ingredients such as cucumber, tomato, onion, parsley, and lemon juice. Oh, for a mountainous slab of charbroiled meat fresh from the kettle grills of *Retreat*. Don't get me wrong. We understood and appreciated, certainly, that main course salad entrees were the best they could manage under the circumstances. Even those simple rations taxed their resources, and we were duly grateful. Nonetheless, to this day, such fare does not appeal to me.

One morning, as the fragile peace seemed to be holding, I received a surprise visitor. Jack Meiseles, a volunteer in the 72nd Battalion infantry, somehow managed to locate me. We had made one another's acquaintance while bivouacked in the Trets training camp. Though he seemed quite happy to see me, I could sense that something was troubling him. After an initial exchange of gosh-it's-good-to-see-you greetings, he became very emotional, to the point of tears.

"What's up, Jack? What's wrong?" I asked.

"Have you seen your passport, Sidney?" he spilled, shaken. I shook my head: *no*. He proceeded to inform me that the Israelis were actually *using* our passports, that our papers were not, as we had assumed all along, being held in safekeeping.

I couldn't believe what I was hearing. I was not irate, but I was indeed upset, because I had a strong gut feeling that what Jack had heard was spot on. Yes, I understood that those in high command leading the *War of Independence* were obliged to employ all means and tools at their disposal to defend the new state and secure its future. But what of *my* future, *after* the war? Lacking a passport, my return to Great Britain would be in jeopardy.

Jack had good reason to feel betrayed and distraught. He was

150

between the proverbial rock and a hard place – a potentially stateless person, neither here nor there, and not for the first time in his life. He had escaped the Nazi peril in 1937, fleeing his birth country for the haven of England. Not being a citizen of Great Britain, he did not qualify for a passport. Instead, local authorities had been decent enough to provide him with the next best thing: papers authorizing overseas travel with right-of-return. Without those papers, Jack – who had never reported them lost or stolen – *might* make it back to England, but only to find himself being deported for the alleged crime of fighting for Israel.

"Can you help me, Sidney?" he asked, choking up. "Can you help me get my papers back?"

With typical wishful thinking and bravado, I assured Jack, "Not to worry, mate. We *will* get our papers back – my passport *and* your visa."

I became a man on a mission. I packed my few belongings and took off at once, heading north, without reporting to the powers-that-be. I had to get answers. I had to get to the bottom of the situation and fix it. The more I thought about it, the more incensed I became. What Jack Meiseles related to me made sense, but that didn't make it acceptable. We were *Machalniks*, not pawns.

The first person with whom I managed to secure an appointment was none other than the commander of the Israeli Air Force, Major General Aharon Remez. We met at his headquarters building, a modest converted bungalow in a residential district of the port city of Jaffa.

He waved me into his sparsely furnished office, indicating that I should take a seat as he did the same from behind his desk, swinging his outstretched legs up on top to assume a comfortable position of authority. "How can I help you?"

"Passports and papers," I replied. "When we, me and my mates, when we signed on, we volunteers from the *Diaspora*, the *Haganah* took our passports for safekeeping. That's what we were told – that they were being held until we needed to get them back. Only now I've learned that they've been used – *are* being used –

by others. We need to get to the bottom of this and find out what's what."

Befitting his relaxed demeanor, Remez downplayed my concerns. "There's a war on. You know that. We do what we need to do. We all make sacrifices. That's part of the price we pay if we want to come out on top."

He professed to have no idea where my passport was or could possibly be, nor to whom or where I might next turn to inquire. With a cursory wave of the hand, he gave me the brushoff. *Nothing we can do. Nothing to be done.*

I left his office in full steam. The commander's behavior was blasé and dismissive. *This is the thanks I get for putting my life on the line?* In essence, Remez had implied that my property was *not* my property, and that, in effect, lacking the means to return to my country, I had become *de facto* an Israeli, with no say in the matter whatsoever. I was more determined than ever to find the person or persons responsible for the disappearance and furtive deployment of my passport.

Later, I would learn that Major General Aharon Remez had himself served in the capacity of a *Machalnik*-like volunteer. Born in Tel Aviv in 1919, he had joined the Haganah in 1936, took flying lessons in the United States, joined the Royal Air Force in 1942, and "flew a Spitfire for Britain in combat against the Germans."[31]

I would also learn that the majority of the volunteers from the *Diaspora* had not been disposed to abandon their birth country, family, and friends – that they, like me, fully intended to return home after playing their part in the *War of Independence*. How many of them might have had the same 'misplaced papers' problem was anyone's guess.

I resolved not to return to my unit in the Negev. Given the stature of my command in the *Tel Litvinsky* training camp, the

---

[31] 'Aharon Remez, 75; Led Israeli Air Force,' *The New York Times* (April 6, 1994).

equivalent of lieutenant colonel, I was able to find suitable lodgings quite readily in an officers quarters billet adjacent to the main air force base. From there, it was a short ride of about ten kilometers north-northeast into central Tel Aviv, where I enjoyed the company of peers once again within that convivial watering hole, Maxim's.

## Of All the Dumb Luck

It happened by chance. I had made an offhand remark to one of the fellows, a passing reference to my 'wandering' passport situation. "I think I may be able to help you," he said, pointing to a pretty young woman sitting nearby. "See her. Her name is Rachel. She works in the local passport office. She's been known to fix one up, if you know what I mean. To do a favor. Not for just anyone, though."

He left it at that. The rest was up to me. Right then and there, I made it my business to have a go at befriending her. I introduced myself and asked if she might be free for lunch. My treat. She accepted. First base.

In no time at all, we were sitting face-to-face over plates of who-gives-a-damn. For her, it might have seemed as if an amiably brash, good-looking Brit was looking to chat her up. For me, however, it was strictly an information-gathering foray. Without much conversational foreplay, I stated my dilemma and pressing need.

Thankfully, she seemed neither surprised nor disappointed. "There's a Mister Liechtenstein," she replied. "His office is around the corner from where you're staying. Go and see him. He should be able to help you."

And so I did. After introducing myself and stating my reason for contacting him, he played the cagy tortoise. "English, I don't speak so good," he claimed. Next, I tried Yiddish, with the same result. He shrugged his shoulders. I knew he understood what I was asking for, but he was using delaying tactics. And so I left, not to give up the chase, but to go and find my ace-in-the-hole, Jack

153

Meiseles. Jack, with his Eastern European roots and working knowledge of German, Yiddish, English, and basic Hebrew, would serve as our barrier-busting interpreter.

Meiseles and I had arranged to maintain contact with one another through one of the fellows who owned and managed Maxim's. Not the most efficient of methods, but effective, nonetheless. "Come join me here, Jack, and we'll tree this fellow together." He joined the hunt with alacrity.

There were two of us now, and Mr. Liechtenstein could see that we meant business. Perhaps he felt some sort of affinity for Jack's background and saga, but in any event the result was what we had been pining for. "Come back tomorrow," he said, speaking in the Yiddish tongue he had feigned not knowing the day before, "and we should be able to supply you with what you need."

We were ecstatic.

The very next day, almost eleven months after I had set foot in Israel, I presented myself at the passport office. My heart was racing with anticipation. By and large, the fighting was over, and I would be going home.

"Take a seat," Liechtenstein invited, "and try not to be upset with me."

"What?!" I exclaimed.

"Look," he explained, reaching across his desk to hand me a British passport, "this is not yours. *Your* passport is in Paris, at the *Jewish Agency*, where you surrendered it. This will get you there, from here to Paris."

As I opened the ersatz booklet to the second page, he calmly told me what I could plainly see for myself. "You're not exactly you, Mr. Fersht. You're a forty-eight-year-old resident of Denmark. Copenhagen, actually. A married man with four children. If you're challenged and asked why *this* passport, you're to tell them that your old one expired, and you managed to arrange to have a new one issued by the consul general's office."

I was astounded. The only thing that belonged to me in the

154

bogus document was my picture – *my* picture, from my very own original passport, which they had obviously removed in order to 'repurpose' it for clandestine operations with someone else's likeness.

Liechtenstein, from his narrow vantage point, had done what he had promised. To boot, he handed to me an envelope with fifteen pounds severance pay and a plane ticket to Paris. *So this is it, after all I've done: a hot passport and a pittance.* I was so incensed, I tore out of his office. I can't remember whether I thanked him, but I should have. He'd done the most he could.

Even so, and sadly, I felt somewhat cut off and let down by the state for which I had put my life on the line. I was on my own, adrift in deep, uncharted waters. Undiminished in my recollection was the manner in which I had been searched before leaving England by the imperious Customs officer and his chill warning: "We *will* get you on your return. Have no doubt."

When I had settled down, I reasoned with myself. The revelation that my original passport had itself gone to war was simply a fact of life. It was up to me to deal with the consequences. There would be no turning back. There was also the heartening consolation via Jack Meiseles that the situation with his papers had been sorted out as well. *So lighten up, Sidney, and get on with it.*

I had managed to save ten pounds sterling on my own. That, together with Mr. Liechtenstein's departing gift of fifteen, enabled me to purchase a made-in-Israel, German-tailored (of all things) grey gabardine raincoat. A genuine beauty.

Heading home meant facing Customs authorities on each of the two legs of the journey. First Paris, then England. Would my likeness, pasted onto a passport purporting to be that of a man twenty years my senior, be my undoing?

After arriving at Lydda Airport, I found myself inadvertently standing in line for a direct flight to London. No way was my passport going to pass muster there. I hastened out of that line with the winged feet of Mercury. And besides, my voucher was for a flight to Paris – on which I did secure a seat as soon as I spotted an

*Air France* departure listed with that destination.

Once airborne, you'd have thought my mind would be preoccupied with all of the what-ifs that lay ahead and their troubling uncertainties. But no, the fate which commanded my attention and that of twenty-something fellow sitting next to me was that of a non-kosher sandwich.

After we had reached cruising altitude, a stewardess proceeded down the aisle, serving scrumptious ham sandwiches. We wolfed them down in nothing flat and fell into conversation. "Gosh, those were good!" and "Sure would be nice to have a second helping." Doesn't matter who said which – we were in complete agreement and began obsessing about another one.

Just then, we noticed that the man in the aisle seat directly ahead of us, clearly an Orthodox Jew, what with his black hat, long black beard and sideburns, and ringlets curled over his ears – he hadn't touched his serving. His tray was down, and the box lunch package was just sitting there, unopened, doing neither him nor us any good.

"Excuse me, Sir," I asked, gaining his attention. "My friend and I – we couldn't help but notice you haven't touched your meal. If you're not planning on eating it, could we have it? Please?"

He eyed me as if I had violated a commandment. Pigs have cloven hooves, but do not chew their cud. Thus are they, according to Old Testament strictures, strictly *verboten*. "Mister," he replied sternly, "if it's not good enough for me, then it's not good enough for you."

There was a certain unassailable logic to his imposition of biblical standards of conduct on us. Instead of being offended, my companion and I got a kick out of it and laughed good-naturedly. It was a relief to have something to lighten the spirits. I needed it.

## Encore de l'Étoile

Customs at *Aéroport de Paris-Orly* must have been a breeze. The fact that I remember nothing of it must mean that my papers, though not kosher (so to speak), had either satisfied the examiners or, given France's having abetted *Aliyah Bet*, that they were willing to turn a blind eye to a returning British soldier in transit to points beyond.

From *Orly*, I headed straight for the *Jewish Agency* offices at *Place de l'Étoile*. There, as before on my outbound journey, I was greeted with a phlegmatic Gallic *Oui, Monsieur.* "I'm here to retrieve my original passport," I said to the reigning clerk. "Here's what your people gave me in Tel Aviv – this temporary phony."

"*Nous voyons*," she replied, taking it from my hand. "Let me see. *Ah, oui, d'accord.* Very well. Come back in a few days. All right?"

It was not all right, and I said so, angrily and loudly.

"But *Monsieur*, there is nothing we can do for you now. You must give us a few days and then come back. *Oui*? And not to worry – we will pay for your hotel."

What were my alternatives? None. "Keep your money," I shot back. "Give it to the next person, someone who might actually need it." Principled to a fault was I. Another instance of speaking emotionally before thinking rationally.

And, alas, not long thereafter, I returned rather sheepishly to the *Jewish Agency*, to ask for help. No hotel would offer me an accommodation without my producing a passport. *Madame Oui d'Accord*, with a trace of a smirk, wrote down and handed to me the address of a cooperating rooming house close by. "Do not go sightseeing. Roaming the streets *sans papiers*, it is not safe. *Ne quittez pas la maison* – stay inside, *Monsieur*, *spécialement* during the day."

What a disappointment. I had so relished the thought of spending my forced three-day 'holiday' taking in, for the second time in my life, the delightful sights, sounds, cuisine, and ambiance of the *City of Lights*, but I had to accept the wisdom of her advice. If I were to be stopped and detained, my problem would also become that of the *Jewish Agency* itself. I had to keep my eye on the prize: returning home to England, safe and sound.

The '*maison*' to which she directed me was a seedy, down-on-the-heels dump. Its narrow corridors were dimly lit and reeked of musty body odor and stale urine. The second floor's communal bathroom featured one throne and a rudimentary washbasin: a bowl perched atop a crude stand, with a pitcher of water alongside.

The worst part was I had to stay in my room during the daylight hours, only going out at night for food. There was nothing else to do, other than give in to obsessing about that meddlesome Irishman. "We *will* get you on your return. Have no doubt."

For hours on end, I assessed the likelihood, back and forth *ad nauseum*, that I might get caught out. Hundreds and thousands of people presented themselves to Customs every day. There simply wasn't enough time for close examinations of each and every one. The odds alone were in my favor. But what if the irascible Irishman had gone further than wagging his finger and threatening me – what if he had gone on to record the name Fersht, Sidney on a watch list of some sort? What if Customs officials, eager to pounce, were on the lookout for incoming British *Machalniks* such as me?

The endless debate regarding the prospect of discovery and imprisonment was making me crazy.  All I wanted was to get it all over with. Every afternoon, like clockwork, I phoned the *Jewish Agency*. "Do you have it? Do you have my passport?" *No … no … no …* and then, thank goodness at last, *yes*.

I flew there in a flash. As *Madame Oui d'Accord* handed it to me, my pulse was pounding. *England*, here I come! I flipped open the cover and *yes*, there was my picture, stuck back inside my original passport. *Hallelujah!* I was twenty-eight again, unmarried and childless. That was the good news. Then my eyes focused on the rest of the story. My picture had been crudely fixed in place, with a thick ribbon of glue congealed around it. It was obvious from contrasting colors on the page that a larger-size photograph had occupied the space where mine now resided. Turning the pages, I found a plethora of visa stamps indicating that I – or, rather, the agent or agents pretending to be me – had crisscrossed foreign borders time and time again.

A magma of outrage rose from my gut. "Just look at this! How in hell do you think I'll be able to get through Customs at Dover without being questioned?"

"*Oui, d'accord.* Good luck, *Monsieur.*"

As I departed the *Jewish Agency*, my head was spinning with the what-ifs again. What if I'm caught? What if they decide to make an example out of me? What if an impostor of Sidney Fersht had committed crimes in my name? What if, what if, what if. I could go to jail. I was upset – *angry* – about the whole situation. Did they even think about that – about the consequences were I to be found out and held accountable?

*Maybe* they were telling the truth when they claimed that the passports they had collected were being held for safekeeping – allegedly to thwart discovery by British military patrols. But at some point, they had decided to employ the passports as fungible assets for use in effecting covert operations.

The fact that we had emerged victorious in the *War of Independence* was some consolation for the pickle they had put me in. We had given our all for a cause we believed in. Whatever disappointment I felt at being left high and dry, at first without a passport and then with one that had been crudely and visibly compromised, was abated by the knowledge that whereas we *Machalniks* had had a choice, indigenous Israelis did not. They were fighting for their lives. My travails were minuscule compared to the perils with which they had to contend.

*How do I crawl out of this mess?*

With all that rattling around in my noggin, I went on a shopping spree. 'Retail therapy' they call it now. I still had a few pounds in my pocket, and back then, a pound was worth umpteen multiples of what it buys today.

First, I treated myself to a plush velour felt fedora, just like the one worn by a popular cinema actor of the era, Adolphe Menjou. Next, I stopped at a kiosk to buy a newspaper – not an English language one, mind you, but French. Why, I haven't a clue. And then, from a fruit vendor, a shiny red apple.

At the ferry terminal, my heart palpitations commenced once more. This was it. No turning back. For no reason in particular, even though I had but one small piece of luggage, I decided to check it through to London's Victoria Station. Perhaps I wanted to be free to walk about the boat without having to mind a suitcase. Or perhaps there was an angel sitting on my shoulder, whispering in my ear.

I folded and tucked the buff-colored checked parcels receipt inside the back cover of my passport, made my way to the departure area, and stood in queue, waiting for my future to be determined.

Once aboard the ferry, I assumed my familiar position at the rail and allowed my thoughts to drift with the movement of the boat. I was a *Machalnik* – an overseas volunteer in Israel's *War of Independence* – returning home for the second time from faraway fields of battle.

As the distance closed between the ferry and the Dover shore, the demarcation line between my having been a faithful warrior in service to my country and then being considered a terrorist by that same proud nation lurched nearer with each thrust and plunge of the bow.

The southern coast of England beckoned on a vast, impermanent horizon. Its chalky cliffs, maritime villages, and expansive strands heaved with each passing wave.

I was gripped by the sensation that the land mass itself was in motion, straining to reach me, to hold me accountable. My feet were wedded to the deck, fixed in place by trepidation. My papers, as the murderous Bosch would say, were not in order. My passport, redeemed from purgatory less than twenty-four hours before, had traveled far and wide without me, bearing other faces, other lives, toward the glory of triumph or the destiny of an early grave.

I was not alone. We were a motley assembly of returnees, many of us, each consumed with the prospect of what comes next. Southern England's shoreline grew nigh. A loudspeaker blasted a shrill warning, assaulting ears and apprehensions: "Those *without*

British passports will be met and interviewed by the local constabulary. Those *with* British passports—*Scotland Yard*."

The announcement precipitated urgent flashes of memory, disparate, yet connected. A social club in the Leytonstone area of London's East End, where representatives of the *Haganah* and the *Palmach*, dispatched as proselytizers and recruiters by David Ben Gurion, exhorted the audience to answer the call and join the fight to defend the newly declared State of Israel. The look of shock and disapproval on the face of my sister Celia, the oldest of nine siblings and twenty-one years my senior, as I declared my intention to leave the country and do my bit to help secure Israel's territorial birthright in the Middle East. The suspicious, self-righteous Customs officer at Dover, who, having searched me and my belongings fruitlessly for overt signs of my intention to become a *Machalnik*, issued that stern threat in dismissing me: "We *will* get you on your return."

Yes, I was returning—from a long, young adulthood spent in harm's way for just causes. From British soil to Cape Town, South Africa. From Bombay to Calcutta and Delhi. From the vast, sweltering RAF staging post at Chittagong to the inhospitable wildernesses of Burma, all the way down to Mandalay. From postwar civilian life under my nation's flag to standard-bearing freedom fighter under another. From celebrated victory in the Jewish homeland to back home in England, where no laurels, parades, or confetti awaited one's return. It would have been folly to expect any such greeting. My only hope, albeit a fervent one, was that on disembarking, I would not be regarded and treated as having been traitorous.

A stubby booklet, well-worn and all too obviously altered, was all that separated me from what transpired before and what would come after. In a larger sense, however, I was not beholden to it. My journey was stamped indelibly, yet invisibly, not only with my own aspirations and adventures, but also with those of my forebears, courageous men and women who had risked all that I might be born into a land free of religious and ethnic persecution. Had it not been for their daring and foresight in fleeing tyranny and oppression, I would not be. I would not have been there to shoulder arms against the scourge of Axis evil and take them up again in defense of the fledgling State of Israel.

As the ferryboat made port and slowed to slip into its dockside berth, my reverie ended and the knots began to grow again in my stomach. I carried a British passport. Scotland Yard awaited.

In descending the boarding ramp, I began to shudder all over. My teeth clattered involuntarily with nervous energy. To occupy and silence them, I took a giant bite of the apple I'd been carrying all the way from Paris and then stuffed the bugger into a pocket.

I tried to look cool as the British-Passports-Only queue advanced. Tucked under my left arm was a copy of the prior day's *Le Monde*. Draped over the forearm was my grey gabardine raincoat, complemented by Adolphe Menjou's fedora in the hand.

"Next!" barked the inspector from Her Majesty's Metropolitan Police Service.

With a stiff upper lip pasted on my face, I extended my right hand to present the wayward passport. The moment of truth was at hand. Panic set in. A clump of apple got lodged in my esophagus. I gagged and coughed, cleared my throat, and croaked, "I've lost my luggage! I've lost my blooming luggage!" Where that came from, I have no idea. I must have sounded desperate and daft.

The inspector took one look at the spectacle standing in front of him, nipped the checked baggage receipt from between the pages of the passport, still held firmly in my right hand, and held the slip up as evidence of my patent stupidity. "You haven't lost your luggage at all, you sod. Look here – you've checked it through to Victoria." He had spotted the buff-colored claim ticket at once, so ubiquitous and familiar were they to the authorities. "Now get on with you!"

*Now get on with you!* Music to my ears. A five-word symphony. Never before or after in my entire life did I move as quickly as I did then.

At the Dover rail station, the stairway to track level was long and steep, descending forever below ground. I believe I did the three-minute mile in less than a minute. It's a wonder I didn't break my neck. Fueled by adrenaline, I marched the length of the platform, up and down several times, exhilarated by my stupendous good fortune. I knew that I needed to calm down, but at the same time, I was loath to dilute the pure elixir of relief, of the shedding at long last of oppressive dread. I was home free, soon to be boarding the next train to Victoria Station, to be reunited once again with family and friends. It was time to celebrate, to cheer my good fortune.

And to thank that angel sitting on my shoulder, whispering in my ear.

# PART THREE
# THIRD FLAG

# CHAPTER 10
# ANOTHER COUNTRY

On March 1, 1967, three weeks before my forty-sixth birthday, I became a naturalized citizen of the United States, proudly taking the ceremonial *Oath of Allegiance*:

> I hereby declare, on oath, that I absolutely and entirely renounce and abjure all allegiance and fidelity to any foreign prince, potentate, state, or sovereignty, of whom or which I have heretofore been a subject or citizen; that I will support and defend the Constitution and laws of the United States of America against all enemies, foreign and domestic; that I will bear true faith and allegiance to the same; that I will bear arms on behalf of the United States when required by the law; that I will perform noncombatant service in the Armed Forces of the United States when required by the law; that I will perform work of national importance under civilian direction when required by the law; and that I take this obligation freely, without any mental reservation or purpose of evasion; so help me God.

Thenceforth, I would salute the *Stars and Stripes*, the third and final flag of my ongoing journey. How had I come to that point? How had I, a child of immigrant parents, born in the United Kingdom, eventually come to seek a new life in one of its former breakaway colonies, becoming thereby an immigrant myself?

My memory of the day I stepped foot on mainland American soil, Wednesday, May 11, 1960, is as indelible as that of my arrival in the port of Tel Aviv aboard the *Monte Chiaro*, stepping down the gangplank to plant my feet on the fresh ground of the new State of Israel.

The vessel that carried and delivered me, my wife of ten years, three-year-old son Vincent, and infant daughter Sara to the U.S.A.

was the stately *SS Statendam* of the Holland America Line.

It was a fair day in the low sixties as the ship approached New York, offering us a glorious view of the storied Statue of Liberty on our way to berth at Pier 40 on the Hudson River side of the city.

As exciting as it was to have made land at melting pot America's largest metropolis, itself a grand aggregation of multitudinous nationalities, ethnicities, and cultures, we looked forward with great anticipation to making our way to our ultimate destination, Philadelphia.

Why America? Why Philadelphia, Pennsylvania? In a word: opportunity.

## Backstory

Eleven years had transpired since that multistage trek returning from service in the Holy Land – a passage marked by nerve-wracking what-ifs and the specter of ruin each step along the way.

In welcoming me back, Celia's joy, as with that of my other siblings, had been tempered by the anxiety they had weathered while I was far away in the thick of it. The Second World War had ended almost four years before, but what followed was precarious peacetime.

Twice within the span of my young adulthood, I had volunteered: once for Great Britain and the defense of our nation's way of life, and once for Israel and the survival of its infancy. Were there yet other causes that might tempt the seasoned veteran and no longer 'baby' Baby Brother to answer the call of duty? To their way of thinking and mine as well, however, it was high time to lay down arms and pick up the responsibilities and obligations of a productive civilian life. The work that I found was, predictably, in garments and tailoring.

One year later, I met, courted, and married Ruth Solomons. Son Vincent was born March 1, 1957; daughter Sara exactly three years later, on March 1, 1960.

In retrospect, the decade of the 1950s seems to have flown by in the blink of an eye. But of course, it did not. The road to earning a living, growing a family, and making the most of one's talents and ambitions was long, rising, and not without its potholes and detours. I persevered and – as always – strived to do more, to be more, to feed the restlessness and resourcefulness that had become engrained in my nature from early on when, sheltered at home and in the backyard, I'd been shielded from the chaotic, uncertain world outside by dear mother Rivka.

As a twenty-eight-year-old ex-serviceman whose teenage years had been spent laboring in the workshops and sweatshops of London's East End furniture factories and rag trade, I could not feature tailoring, and only that, for the rest of my life. I furthered my education by taking a course in pattern-making and secured a job as such in Northampton – to gain experience so that one day I might qualify for more prestigious and remunerative positions back in London.

With marriage came in-laws – and happily so. Ruth's aunt on her mother's side, Doris, and her husband Hyman Genyon, had emigrated to America sometime in the late 1940s to early 1950s, making their home in Philadelphia. Knowing of my yearning to expand my family's horizons and opportunities for learning and advancement, they made the case for our taking the plunge as well and moving to where the legendary streets were paved with gold.

It was not a decision to be made lightly. Though I had experienced diverse cultures in Europe, Africa, the Far East, and the Middle East, it was as a transient soldier, not as a prospective immigrant. England had been my home, having taken in my asylum-seeking parents. The country of my birth was all I really knew, and I knew it to be fiercely proud and resilient.

Great Britain, under siege, had beaten back the Nazi onslaught in concert with America, an alliance lauded by Winston Churchill as a "special relationship between the British Commonwealth and

Empire and the United States."[32] George Bernard Shaw was reported to have said they were "two countries separated by a common language." I had to wonder whether a Cockney such as I, born and bred within the sound of the bells of Christopher Wren's grand Church of St. Mary-le-Bow, would be able to make a go of it as a newbie in the melting pot, as a sort of manual laborer, albeit a skilled one, in a highly competitive field.

"It's now or never," I said to myself, proceeding from gut and gusto as was my way, but the decision was not mine alone to make. Thankfully, Ruth understood and appreciated my desire to reach higher.

"Once we decide to go," I ventured, "there will be no turning back. We need to be fully committed, Ruth, if we're to succeed."

Ruth's brother Irving, who had himself emigrated to the Philadelphia area in the mid-1950s, became our sponsor and benefactor. Aunt Doris arranged for us to reside in a rented home, with three months prepaid.

Immediately, on our very first Monday in America, I set out to find suitable work, heading downtown to respond to a help-wanted classified advertisement for a cutter in the garment industry. Though I lacked the formal credentials for such a position, that didn't stop me. The pay was seventy dollars per week in a non-union shop. So be it. I would be earning, and it was a point of honor for me that I redeem my indebtedness to others with all due dispatch.

Toward that end, I also established my own side business, operating from home: performing alternations, at which I was superbly adept. My workshop, such as it was, consisted of tables and platforms fashioned from the crates in which our worldly possessions had been shipped, along with the fundamental machinery of the tools of the trade. Soon I was pulling in more

---

[32] Source: From an address delivered March 5, 1946, by Winston Churchill (then Leader of the Opposition) at Westminster College, Fulton, Missouri. Historians refer to the address as Churchill's 'Iron Curtain Speech.'

money than was needed to pay the bills – while burning the candle at both ends.

Industriousness and perseverance were the hallmarks of my efforts to build a better life and future for me and our family. Over the course of the several years that followed, I progressed to more responsible and remunerative positions with major local makers of higher end women's clothing. I began investing in residential and commercial real estate holdings. And I arranged to fund establishment of a boutique ladies' dress shop run by Ruth and Aunt Doris.

Along the way, on August 29, 1961, our family grew with the birth of son Robert.

The 1960s were years of plenty, and life was good. We were safe and secure, working hard and prospering, and living the American dream.

There would be no turning back.


## Life Goes On

In the mid-1970s, for reasons we need not address in this memoir, Ruth and I separated and divorced. Our union had produced three wonderful, beautiful children. Together, we had embraced and enjoyed the great adventure of America. The streets were not paved with gold, but the opportunities were golden. There was much for which to be thankful.

In 1979, at the age of fifty-eight, neither remarriage nor romance were on my mind or on the horizon when I met Selma Redner, a lovely woman who had lost her husband far too young in life. The occasion was a blind date arranged by one of her well-meaning friends. As Selma relates it, she was dubious regarding yet another 'you ought to meet so-and-so' pairing, especially this time with a divorced Englishman eight years her senior. She insisted that the chemistry test be conducted over casual cups of coffee, *not* dinner, so as to facilitate her bailing out nicely and neatly if she so desired.

The year 2019 marked our fortieth wedding anniversary.

With our extended families – including daughter Carole Lukoff and spouse Joel, daughter Sara Minkoff and spouse Jay, son Vincent and spouse Jane, and son Robert – Selma and I are blessed. We are proud parents and grandparents, and in reasonably good health considering we are up there in years. There isn't a day goes by that we don't repeat the words: "How grateful are we for the lives we live."

\

\

# CHAPTER 11
# 1988 MACHAL REUNION

Purely by happenstance, I became aware of concurrent events planned for the fortieth anniversary celebration of the birth of the State of Israel and the reunion of its *Machalnik* forces.

One evening, Selma and I had a *shiva* call to make to the family of one of her Hadassah friends, Rose Marmelstein, whose father had passed away. During the course of our visit, I fell into conversation with Rose's husband, Phillip, whom I had not met previously. He had served as a U.S. Navy pilot during World War II *and* had volunteered to pilot aircraft in Israel's *War of Independence*, transporting bombers from Europe to Israel in 1948. The next year, he flew for *Operation Magic Carpet*, a secretive undertaking that airlifted tens of thousands oppressed Jews from North Africa to Israel.

Phillip knew I had served in the *Haganah*. He informed me that the war's veteran overseas volunteers, we *Machalniks*, were to be honored on the occasion of Israel's fortieth anniversary. Acting on his recommendation, I became a member of the *Machal* organization, established to memorialize our contributions and, eventually, to serve as a networking tool.

The invitation to attend the *International Machal Convention* came in the form of a letter from one of Israel's foremost military leaders, Yitzhak Rabin, Minister of Defense and former Prime Minister.

As I held the letter in my hand, a torrent of thoughts and feelings came flooding in. Forty years. Could it really have been that long ago? I could close my eyes and picture *Tel Litvinsky* that very first night. Forty years had been only one yesterday.

171

## *El Al* to Tel Aviv

Within the *El Al* terminal security holding area at New York's JFK Airport, I joined a group of senior citizens, men and women, each with identical labels fastened to their luggage. Excitement and lighthearted camaraderie began immediately as we introduced ourselves to one another. The spouse of one *Machalnik* popped open a bottle of Champagne to initiate the celebration of our return to the Holy Land.

Bubbly conviviality continued throughout the boarding process and held sway throughout the flight. Once the plane had reached cruising altitude and we were permitted to walk about the cabin, several Orthodox Jews gathered at the rear of the aircraft to join in morning prayers. We were traveling as one to the capital of the country we had helped to save and secure, *Israel. Blessèd Israel*.

What we didn't realize until we had landed at Ben Gurion Airport is that we were about to be treated as VIPs. On the ground, cameramen awaiting our arrival began snapping pictures from the moment we exited the plane. A CBS-affiliated reporter traveling with us had interviewed one of our own for a piece that would air on Charles Kuralt's *Sunday Morning* program.

We were directed to modern, commodious motor coaches as baggage handlers transferred our luggage from the jetliner's cargo hold to the buses' side panel storage bins. We had not been on the road for very long when the caravan stopped unexpectedly. We could hear music playing nearby as a dignified fellow from another coach boarded ours and introduced himself as the Mayor of Kiryat Ono, a community located approximately ten kilometers east of central Tel Aviv. "We are escorting you to town, ladies and gentlemen, where our youth symphony orchestra will welcome you officially to Israel."

The atmosphere was electrifying as, from a balcony overlook, we gazed down upon the school-age children poised to honor us with music. You could tell from their worshipful faces that they had been fully briefed regarding the role we had played in helping to secure their homeland. They played with heart for the crusading

172

guardian angels arrayed above, *Machalniks* for whom the intervening forty years seemed to melt away.

## Honored to be Honored

At each stop that day and the nine that followed, planned events and displays either paid homage or related to our service. Arriving at the Palmachim Airbase on the Mediterranean coast, one half hour south of Kiryat Ono, we were met by a lovely female officer who presented each of us with flowers. As at most stops on our tour, there were beverages and fresh fruits to welcome us as well. The base commander had a treat in store. Fighter crews sped by Jeep to the airfield, where their respective *Douglas A-4 Skyhawk* birds of prey had been prepped for take-off. They boarded them swiftly, brought their engines to full throttle, and zoomed off with the roar of glorious rolling thunder. Once airborne, they assembled in formation, aviated in long, looping, graceful circuits around the circumference of the base, and dipped their wings in salute. We were deeply moved to be so honored.

Our itinerary was jam-packed. At the next stop, also a military base, a leader of the Israeli Armored Corps invited us to break bread with resident tank crews. Afterwards, they served up a demonstration of action station firepower, blowing to smithereens a target one-tenth of a mile downrange. I recall having asked their commandant if there was a maximum height for personnel assigned to operate such fearsome machines. "We take whatever we can get," came the candidly pragmatic reply.

At the Ashdod Naval Base, a short drive further south along the coast, we toured a state-of-the-art high-tech, heavily armed gunboat, one of a fleet of relatively small warships designed for speedy hit-and-run maneuverability. Even then, thirty years ago, computerized tracking and guidance systems enabled virtually instantaneous response to threat targets.

## Reverence and Remembrance

Having traveled about sixty-five kilometers due east, we found ourselves standing at the shrine of the *Dome of the Rock* at Temple

Mount in Jerusalem's Old City. The site has deep meaning for people of three monotheistic faiths – Islamic, Jewish, and Christian. Why then, I asked myself at the time, given that we share the common ground of belief in a higher being and the earth beneath our feet, do we allow bigotry, discrimination, and worse to infect our humanity?

Across the city to the west was *Yad Vashem*, The World Holocaust Remembrance Center. We entered a room lit only by candlelight, where a dulcet recorded voice intoned the names of each child murdered by the Nazis. The effect was chilling – and profoundly disturbing. I could feel my blood pressure rising. Had it not been for my grandparents' and parents' foresight and courage, my name, too, might be among those being chanted within the hallowed walls of the center. With humility, my heart ached to breaking for those who had met such a heinous fate.

At the *Western Wall*, as was the custom observed by most tourist visitors, I penned a note and inserted it in a tight crevice between the stones forming the structure. What I wrote is long lost to the ebb of memory, but I'd like to think, given the life I've been fortunate to lead before and after, that my prayers had been granted.

## We *Machalniks*

To use the vernacular of my adoptive country, the journey of reunion was a blast from beginning to end. People who had lost touch with one another met, exchanged stories of four decades of lives lived in-between, and bonded again as the years apart evaporated.

Mark Compton, fellow volunteer who had shared the Trets training camp experience with me, had remained in Israel, married, and raised a family. Mark owned a furniture store, served as a sergeant in his community's militia, and – no surprise – performed a lot of volunteer work.

Mark passed away a few years later, God rest his soul. When his son informed me of his death, he mailed to me his very own

Israeli Defense Force badges, knowing that as *Machalniks*, neither his father nor I (nor any other overseas volunteer) had been issued such emblems of service in the *War of Independence*. Like father, like son: thoughtful, reverent, and true.

Another highlight of the journey was meeting Jack 'Freddy' Freedman for the first time. We soon found out that we were *landsmen* – in Yiddish, close neighbors – in that he resided in London's Shoreditch borough, about ten minutes' walk from where I had been born and raised in the East End. Our affinity did not stop there. Like me, he, too, at the age of fourteen had had his formal education truncated as his mother lay dying, with his father gone. Her last words were to implore him to join the RAF, learn a trade, and help his younger brother get a leg up on life when *his* turn came to leave school and enter the world.

In due course, Freddy did join the RAF, where he became a stellar aircraft engineer. Eventually, he was shipped overseas to serve Great Britain's interests in Mandatory Palestine. From the previously cited treatise on the *Machal* by Dr. Yaacov Markovitzky, we have the following testimonial to Freddy's invaluable contribution to the cause:

> Jack Freedman (Ya'acov "Freddy" Ish-Shalom), of Britain, secretly helped the Haganah's Air Service while still a member of the RAF. In February 1948 he [left] the RAF, after 11 years of service, and joined the Air Service, bringing with him vital experience and expertise in airplane maintenance and overhauling. He headed the team that restored most of the 20 former RAF Auster light airplanes that had been bought from the British as scrap. He also set up and supervised the team that built the Israel Air Force's first Spitfire from scrapped airplanes the British had abandoned when they left Palestine. Perhaps his most important contribution, however, was making his vast technical knowhow available to the young aircraft mechanics he trained, many of whom later assumed key positions of command.

Known to me are so many other fellow *Machalniks*, living and passed, who answered the call. Among them are:

- Leon 'Lee' Silverman, an Israeli Air Force (IAF) intelligence officer. Born in Cleveland, now a Californian, Leon is a fellow with whom I have stayed in contact.
- Irwin 'Swifty' Schindler, an IAF officer who served in the Air Transport Command.
- Hank Greenspun, a Haganah operative.
- Joseph 'Joe' Landow, an Israeli Army Logistics officer.
- Alvin 'Al' Ellis, who served in the Israeli Navy's *Shayetet 13*, a reconnaissance unit.

Profiles of and references to these fine individuals can be found within the online pages of the World Machal website (http://www.machal.org.il/). What did we and all other *Machalniks* have in common? By now in this memoir, you know the answer to that question. Here is how Dr. Markovitzky puts it:

There are as many personal stories about overseas volunteers, and as many factors that motivated them, as the number of countries from which they came. Primarily, they were motivated by Jewish solidarity and concern for the security of the small *Yishuv* in its struggle for survival. Most had been soldiers in the armies of their countries of origin during World War II and felt the need to offer their military experience, skills and technical knowhow. Some were members of Zionist youth movements.

They came with a sense of mission, with feelings of pride and privilege, knowing they were helping to create a state and defend a Jewish homeland. Some, including non-Jews, were moved by the plight of the Jewish people. They had witnessed the calamity of the Holocaust and wanted to come to the aid of the beleaguered *Yishuv*.

For some, their participation in the *Yishuv*'s struggle was an expression of their anger at the British Empire and of anti-imperialism in general. Others believed that an independent and strong State of Israel was essential for the Western countries' need to maintain a presence to protect their interests in this important strategic region. And there were some who were motivated by a sense of adventure.

## Official Acknowledgement

While official acknowledgements by State of Israel of the role of *Machalniks* in the defense of its being have been appropriately laudatory through the years, none to my way of thinking had come close to the threshold of declaring the absolutely *existential* value of the *Machal*. None had, that is, until quite recently.

On May 5, 2019, the *53rd Annual Mickey Marcus Memorial Service* was convened at West Point, the United States Military Academy. Years ago, I attended one such service there and was given the high honor of calling the names of those overseas volunteers who made the supreme sacrifice during Israel's *War of Independence*.

Who was Mickey Marcus? A *Machalnik*. From the website of the *Jewish Virtual Library*:[33]

> David Daniel Mickey Marcus, a tough Brooklyn street kid, rose by virtue of his courage and intelligence to help save Israel in 1948 and become its first general since Judah Maccabee. After a distinguished career in military and public service to the United States, the 46-year-old Marcus wrote his name forever in the annals of Israeli history.
>
> Born to immigrant parents in 1902, Marcus grew up in the Brownsville section of Brooklyn where, to defend himself against neighborhood toughs, he learned to box. His high school athletic and academic record won him admission to West Point in 1920, from which he graduated with

---

[33] Source: *Jewish Virtual Library*,
<https://www.jewishvirtuallibrary.org/mickey-marcus>.

impressive scores. After completing his required service, Marcus went to law school and spent most of the 1930s as a Federal attorney in New York, helping bring Lucky Luciano to justice. As a reward, Mayor LaGuardia named Marcus Commissioner of Corrections for New York City.

Convinced that war was imminent, Marcus voluntarily went back into Army uniform in 1940, and after the Japanese attack on Pearl Harbor served as executive officer to the military governor of Hawaii. In 1942, he was named commandant of the Army's new Ranger school, which developed innovative tactics for jungle fighting. Sent to England on the eve of D-Day, he voluntarily parachuted into Normandy with the troops of the 101st Airborne Division. Marcus helped draw up the surrender terms for Italy and Germany and become part of the occupation government in Berlin. Admiring colleagues identified him as one of the War Department's best brains. He had a bright future ahead of him as a member of the Army's top brass.

In 1944, Marcus's consciousness of himself as a Jew took a dramatic turn when he was put in charge of planning how to sustain the starving millions in the regions liberated by the Allied invasion of Europe. A major part of his responsibilities involved clearing out the Nazi death camps. Here, Marcus came face to face with the survivors of Nazi atrocities and saw with his own eyes the piles of uncounted Jewish corpses in Europe's death camps.

Following that assignment, Marcus was named chief of the War Crimes Division, planning legal and security procedures for the Nuremberg trials. Through these experiences, Marcus came to understand the depths of European anti-Semitism. Though never previously a Zionist, Marcus became convinced that the only hope for the remnants of European Jewry lay in a Jewish homeland in Palestine.

In 1947, Marcus returned to civilian life. A few months later, the United Nations authorized the partition of Palestine and the eventual creation of a

Jewish state. Within days, David Ben-Gurion asked Marcus to recruit an American officer to serve as military advisor to Israel. Failing in his attempts to recruit one of his friends, Marcus decided to volunteer himself. The U.S. War Department granted Marcus, who was a reservist, permission to accept the offer, provided Marcus not use his own name or rank and disguise his military record.

Thus, one "Michael Stone" arrived in Tel Aviv in January 1948, to confront a nearly impossible situation. The widely separated Jewish settlements in Palestine were surrounded by a sea of hostile Arabs. The newly created Israel would have no defensible borders, no air power, a few tanks and ancient artillery pieces and almost no arms or ammunition. The Haganah was an effective underground organization but it had no experience as a regular national army. Facing it were well-supplied Arab armies determined to drive the Jews into the sea. The pro-Arab British administration in Palestine prevented the importation of military supplies to the Israelis.

Undaunted, Stone designed a command structure for Israel's new army and wrote manuals to train it, adapting his experience at Ranger school to the Haganah's special needs. He identified Israel's weakest points as the scattered settlements in the Negev and the new quarter of Jerusalem. When Israel declared independence and the Arab armies attacked in May 1948, Israel was ready, thanks to Stone's planning. His hit-and-run tactics kept the Egyptian army in the Negev off balance. When the Jewish section of Jerusalem was about to fall, Marcus ordered the construction of a road to bring additional men and equipment to break the Arab siege just days before the United Nations negotiated a cease fire. Israel had withstood the Arab assault with its borders virtually intact. In gratitude, Ben-Gurion named

179

Marcus a Lieutenant General, the first general in the army of Israel in nearly two thousand years.

Tragically, Marcus did not live to see the peace. Six hours before the cease fire began, in the village of Abu Ghosh near Jerusalem, Marcus was unable to sleep. He walked beyond the guarded perimeter wrapped in his bed sheet. A Jewish sentry saw a white-robed figure approaching and, not understanding Marcus's response, fired a single, fatal shot. Marcus's body was flown back for burial at West Point, where his tombstone identifies him as "A Soldier for All Humanity." Hollywood would later immortalize Marcus in a movie, "Cast A Giant Shadow." Ben-Gurion put it simply, "He was the best man we had."

At the remembrance ceremony, Lieutenant General Gadi Eisenkot, Chief of General Staff of the Israeli Defense Forces, presented the following testimonial:

I wish to express my most sincere appreciation for all the soldiers of the Machal who, with courage, determination and boundless devotion fought in the hardest battles of the War of Independence.

The volunteers of 1948 chose to join our ranks from a shared belief in the righteousness of our cause. They stood determined to the face of the enemy for the sake of ensuring the independence of Israel. The bravery and deep sense of purpose that guided them, as well as their personal experience and professional skills are the foundation upon which the Israel Defense Forces are built until this day. As they stood steadfast in the line of fire, before them lay the dream of 2,000 years: the establishment of a national home for the Jewish people in the Land of Israel.

The soldiers of Machal, who gathered from every corner of the world and tied their fates to the people of this land, left a legacy that guides us to this day. We continue to walk in their footsteps as we work to fulfill our mission: to protect the State of Israel, to secure its existence, and, if necessary, to triumph in war.

In my name and in the name of the soldiers and officers of the IDF, I salute you!

# Chapter 12
# What are the Odds?

On December 1, 2015, Selma and I became residents of *Shannondell at Valley Forge*, a senior living community situated in Audubon, Pennsylvania, about nineteen miles northwest of center city Philadelphia. Included in Shannondell's many features and amenities are movie theaters, one in each of the property's two multi-purpose clubhouses. Approximately two weeks after we moved in, Selma attended an airing of *Above and Beyond*, Nancy Spielberg's cinematic homage to *Machalniks* who had served in the Israeli Air Force:

> In 1948, just three years after the liberation of Nazi death camps, a group of Jewish American pilots answered a call for help. In secret and at great personal risk, they smuggled planes out of the U.S., trained behind the Iron Curtain in Czechoslovakia and flew for Israel in its War of Independence. As members of Machal – "volunteers from abroad" – this ragtag band of brothers not only turned the tide of the war; they also embarked on personal journeys of discovery and renewed Jewish pride.[34]

Sitting next to Selma was Norma Mayron, a member of Shannondell's *Jewish Interest Group*, which had arranged for the film to be shown. Selma had heard of Norma from a mutual acquaintance. When the house lights came up afterwards, Norma happened to remark, "My husband, David, was there."

"Mine, too," Selma replied. "Sidney was in the *Haganah*."

---

[34] Source: *Above and Beyond: The Untold True Story*
<https://aboveandbeyondthemovie.com/about>.

"As was mine!" Norma exclaimed. Both were amazed and excited by the coincidence. An evening meal foursome in the Bradford Clubhouse dining room soon followed.

Early on during that supper, I mentioned that the *Haganah* had posted me to *Tel Litvinsky*, where I served as a training officer. David's face blossomed into a broad smile of awestruck realization. "Oh, my goodness. I was there, too – first in the *Battle for Tel Litvinsky* in March of 1948. Then again later that year."[35]

We determined that we had both been there for a while at the same time, sometime after the *Monte Chiaro* had delivered me to Palestine in late July.

"Now that I think about it," David continued, "looking at you, listening to your voice – your one hundred percent Cockney voice – you and I had to have crossed paths. Because there was an Englishman there, your spitting image, who went out of his way to explain the Cockney language to me. Not only that, I'm pretty sure I have a picture of you somewhere, which you even signed on the back!"

What were the odds? Incalculable, but probably hundreds of millions to one. And yet there we were, both veterans of the Israeli *War of Independence*, comrades-in-arms who had followed our own respective stars and paths for sixty-seven years, only to meet again seven time zones away from yesteryears' fields of battle in a special place we now call home.

David and I share a bond that will survive us. It is a legacy: the State of Israel. *Amen.*

---

[35] 'Towards of the end of the British Mandate of Palestine, Arabs under the command of Hasan Salama began smuggling in arms and personnel disguised as laborers into the camp. The Haganah command saw this as a threat and on April 15, 1948, two companies for the 32nd and 33rd Battalions of the Alexandroni Brigade entered and captured the base.' Source: *Wikipedia*.

# Chapter 13
# One Vote

On Sunday afternoon, November 4, 2018, suffering from increasingly nauseating and painful malaise that seemed to be emanating from my digestive tract, I was taken by ambulance to the *Einstein Medical Center* five miles northeast of *Shannondell*. The issue turned out to be a gall bladder attack.

I am no stranger to hospitals. You don't get to be my age without having organs, joints, and other body parts go on the blink. I have survived heart bypass surgery and, as Shakespeare's *Hamlet* ruminated, "the thousand natural shocks that flesh is heir to." My faith in the medical community is strong. I knew that whatever was wrong with me, they would fix it. There was really only one thing preying on my mind: whether and how I would be able to cast my vote in the election two short days away.

Any thoughts of my being discharged on or before that upcoming Tuesday were dashed by the medical powers-that-be. There were tests to be run and then a bile duct to be cleaned out – on *hospital* time, which, as we well know, always runs in slow motion.

"Selma," I declared, "I *must* vote. There must be a way for me to cast my vote."

Selma phoned the residence of Ann and Bob Goodman. Bob volunteers as a Democratic Party committeeperson for the Lower Providence Township in which our community is situated. He had expended every effort to educate the electorate regarding the issues at hand and to elicit their commitment to vote on voting day. He had arranged for certain candidates running for state and federal offices to 'barnstorm' *Shannondell*: Joe Webster for District 150 of the Pennsylvania House of Representatives; Katie Muth for

District 44 of the Pennsylvania State Senate; and Madeleine Dean for Pennsylvania's 4th District in the U.S. House of Representatives. Surely Bob Goodman would be able to do something.

The next day, Monday, November 5, proved to be challenging and nerve-wracking for all involved in helping me to achieve my unwavering objective: to cast my vote. In order for that to happen, a municipal court judge would need to approve an *Emergency Application for Absentee Ballot*, a special petition required for anyone seeking to submit an absentee ballot "After 5 P.M. on the Friday Before the Primary or Election."

Even that seemingly relatively straightforward task became frustrated and impeded by a circus of unfavorable turns of events. I was in and out of my hospital room for tests and treatments. The first bile duct cleansing had not been successful. Another purge was needed. The hospital's in-house notary refused to validate the *Emergency Application*. As neither I nor Selma was in possession of my driver's license, the notary could not and would not authenticate my identity.

Bob Goodman asked her to pen a note to that effect on the back of the form so that the judge would understand why a non-certified application was being submitted. She did acquiesce to do that much, although even that attestation she declined to notarize.

Time was of the essence, as it was already mid-afternoon and the Montgomery County municipal building housing voter services and the jurisdictional court would be closing for the day at 4 p.m.

Goodman, with the imperfect application in hand, sped to the municipal building four miles away at One Montgomery Plaza in Norristown. His first stop was at the Department of Voter Services on the 6th floor, where he pled his case with one of their staff attorneys. The fellow listened attentively, was won over, and became an advocate. "Let me see if I can find a precedent," he said, leaving the anteroom to research one in the law library.

Five minutes passed. Then ten, fifteen, and twenty as Goodman nervously checked his watch repeatedly as the last grains of sand in the fateful hourglass drained away. It was just after 4 p.m. when the attorney emerged triumphant. "Got it!"

They hurried to the elevator and pressed the button for the 3rd floor courtrooms. Nothing. They tried again and again as the elevator descended all the way to the lobby. With municipal services having closed for the day, the system had been programmed to go into exit-only mode. From the lobby, they climbed the stairs to the third floor stairwell landing and pounded on the door. No one heard them. They huffed and puffed back up to the sixth floor, were admitted by a security officer, and tried the elevator again. This time, although the third floor button did not light, the doors opened there to admit a departing employee. A miracle. The attorney and Goodman fled the car, entered the courtroom, and implored a court clerk to locate the judge.

"Let me do all the talking," the attorney advised Goodman as they waited.

Five minutes on, the judge emerged from chambers. The attorney presented the application and stated the case succinctly. "Plus, Your Honor, I have found a precedent."

The judge raised his hand as if to say 'wait just a moment' as he studied the affidavit and the identity-issue explanation scribed by the notary. "So … tell me if I've got this right. We have a ninety-seven year-old man in hospital who wants to vote. Is that it?"

"Yes, Your Honor. And I have –"

"Ninety-seven, and he wants to vote? Then what are we all doing here? Of course, let him vote! Approved."

"Thank you, Your Honor. Now as to the precedent –"

The judge stood to leave. "Counselor, you need to learn to take *yes* for an answer."

On the morning of Wednesday, November 7, the day after the election during which I had signed the absentee ballot while recuperating on my hospital bed and smiled contentedly as Bob Goodman left to deliver it to *Voter Services*, he came in to share the good news. "Sidney," he said, "You'll be pleased to know that Joe, Katie, and Madeleine won their elections – each by a margin of one vote."[36]

We had a good, hearty laugh. Of course, he was pulling my leg, but it was his way of saying that every vote counts, and that my insistence on finding a way to cast my vote had captured the imaginations and dedication of earnest people who had helped to make it happen.

Why had I been so insistent? It wasn't ego. It was good citizenship. Democracy depends on participation. The issues of the day were too important for me – for any one individual – to abdicate their civic responsibility. Thanks to Selma, Bob, a sympathetic attorney, a clear-thinking judge, and others who combined to secure my right to vote, I did.

---

[36] Joseph Webster carried the district by 3,334 votes, with a margin of 56.0%. Katie Muth by 4,749 votes, with a margin of 52.0%. Madeleine Dean by 90,057 votes, with a margin of 63.5%.

# CHAPTER 14
# THE DISEASE OF ANTI-SEMITISM

David Brooks, a columnist appearing in *The New York Times*, made the following statement in a thoughtful piece entitled 'How to Fight Anti-Semitism' published on March 24, 2019[37]:

> Anti-Semitism is rising around the world. So the question becomes: What can we do to fight it? Do education campaigns work, or marches or conferences? There are three major strains of anti-Semitism circulating, different in kind and virulence, and requiring different responses.

Brooks addressed the distinctions between what he has characterized as 'strains' of anti-Semitism in the Middle East, Europe, and the United States:

> • In the Middle East, anti-Semitism has the feel of a deranged theoretical system for making sense of a world gone astray.

> • In Europe, anti-Semitism looks like a response to alienation.

> • The United States is also seeing a rise in the number of anti-Semitic incidents. But this country remains an astonishingly non-anti-Semitic place. America's problem is the number of people who can't fathom what anti-Semitism is or who think Jews are being paranoid or excessively playing the victim.

---

[37] Source: David Brooks, 'How to Fight Anti-Semitism,' *The New York Times* (Mar. 24, 2019) < https://www.nytimes.com/2015/03/24/opinion/david-brooks-how-to-fight-anti-semitism.html >.

He concluded his remarks by observing:

Groups fighting anti-Semitism sponsor educational campaigns and do a lot of consciousness-raising. I doubt these things do anything to reduce active anti-Semitism. But they can help non-anti-Semites understand the different forms of the cancer in our midst. That's a start.

Eleven days later, also in *The New York Times*, another contributor, Patrick Kingsley, said this[38]:

Swastikas daubed on a Jewish cemetery in France. An anti-Semitic political campaign by Hungary's far-right government. Labour lawmakers in Britain quitting their party and citing ingrained anti-Semitism. A Belgian carnival float caricaturing Orthodox Jews sitting on bags of money.

And that was just the past few months.

The accumulated incidents in Europe and the United States have highlighted how an ancient prejudice is surging in the 21st century in both familiar and mutant ways, fusing ideologies that otherwise would have little overlap.

The spike is taking place in a context of rising global economic uncertainty, an emphasis on race and national identity, and a deepening polarization between the political left and right in Europe and the United States over the conflict between Israel and the Palestinians.

And then, on May 26, 2019, The New York Times put an exclamation point on the phenomenon of anti-Semitic resurgence through an editorial titled 'The Old Scourge of Anti-Semitism Rises Anew in Europe.' Statistical evidence of the sharp rise in old

---

[38] Source: Patrick Kingsley, 'Anti-Semitism Is Back, From the Left, Right and Islamist Extremes. Why?' The New York Times (Apr. 4, 2019) <https://www.nytimes.com/2019/04/04/world/europe/antisemitism-europe-united-states.html >.

hatreds is shockingly alarming. The piece concludes with the following alert and call to action:

All this is not news to European Jews, who for some time have been feeling less and less safe and welcome in their home countries. After polling more than 16,000 Jews in 12 European countries at the end of last year, the European Union's Agency for Fundamental Rights concluded that anti-Semitic hate speech, harassment and fear of being recognized as Jews were becoming the new normal. Eighty-five percent of the respondents thought anti-Semitism was the biggest social and political problem in their countries; almost a third said they avoided Jewish events or sites because of safety concerns. More than a third said they had considered emigrating in the five years preceding the survey.

As appalling as these statistics should be to every European, they should also ring a loud alarm for every American leader of conscience. Speak up, now, when you glimpse evidence of anti-Semitism, particularly within your own ranks, or risk enabling the spread of this deadly virus.

David Brooks and *The New York Times* nailed it: *A cancer in our midst. A deadly virus.* "Speak up now."

I have encountered that cancer, that virus, that pernicious disease, at numerous times, places, and circumstances throughout my life. It is stressful, to say the least, to witness that disease gaining strength. If we are to derive any value from recognizing the phenomenon, any value whatsoever, it is in the knowledge that evil never rests. And sadly, that knowledge is nothing new to learn. It is as old as the Holy Bible and older than that.

At the outset of this memoir, I asked the question 'Why This Memoir?' and asserted "the imperative to act on principle and answer the inner call of duty." I now conclude this journey of remembrance and reflection by addressing that imperative and what it means to me in the context of the state of the world today.

# CHAPTER 15
# CALL OF DUTY

Standing at my hospital bedside on that Sunday, November 4, 2018, Selma did not need to ask me why I was being so insistent that a way be found to enable me to cast my vote. She knew, because she knows me, but I voiced my reason anyway: "They say one vote can make a difference, and with what's happening in America, my one vote might make a *big* difference."

Though quite distinct in terms of circumstances and scale, that determination was akin to the act of conscience which led me to volunteer as a *Machalnik*. I could not and would not leave fighting the good fight to someone else. The sum of such relinquishments of responsibility would doom democracy, liberty, and justice.

The title of this work is *Allegiance Under Three Flags*. As recounted previously herein, I became a naturalized citizen of the United States on March 1, 1967. The *Oath of Allegiance* includes the following pledge:

> I will support and defend the Constitution and laws of the United States of America against all enemies, foreign and domestic, [and] I will bear true faith and allegiance to the same.

I took and take that pledge with utter seriousness and devotion. *Support* and *defend* are action verbs. Bearing true faith and allegiance requires one to *do* something in the face of threat.

I look at the world today and perceive a tide of threats, both foreign and domestic, to decency, justice, charity, equal opportunity – and to the institutions and levers of those democracies which safeguard them.

So long as I am able to draw breath and act in defense of liberty, I will continue to answer the inner call of duty.

Made in the USA
Middletown, DE
28 April 2021